MANAGING PERSONAL DEVELOPMENT

MANAGING PERSONAL DEVELOPMENT

David Turner

The Industrial Society

First published in 1996 by
The Industrial Society
Robert Hyde House
48 Bryanston Square
London W1H 2EA
Telephone: 0870 400 1000

Reprinted January 2001

ISBN 1 85835 431 5

British Library Cataloguing-in-Publication Data.
A catalogue record for this book is available from the British Library

Typeset by: GCS
Printed by: Optichrome, Woking
Cover Design: Rhodes Design

The Industrial Society is a Registered Charity No. 290003

Reference: 1486tw1.01

Contents

Foreword

Training and personal development has finally come through. It is no longer the poorest of poor relations in the world of employment and management. If you are employed by a modern, progressive organisation today, you should be able to look forward with confidence to furthering your personal development. You should recognise that you are going to be more fortunate than those who have gone before. You are likely to be given greater opportunities to pursue more extensive personal development, to a considerably higher standard, than any of your predecessors ever did.

Organisations today are using lots of different approaches to achieve genuine personal development, either to cope with forthcoming change or to equip themselves and their staff with additional skills and competences. The traditional formal course, led by a trainer, still has a certain place, but its pre-eminence has faded. The newer, more comprehensive approach to personal development more often utilises less formal methods. Seeking an effective combination of informality and practicality, many companies are encouraging their staff to use work itself as the main medium for learning and development. Highly effective work-based activities and experiences can be devised, either by the individual or by his or her manager and these can be supported by the use of rewarding self-study materials, including books, audiotapes and videos. Whilst such materials are comfortably familiar, readily available and relatively inexpensive, state-of-the art information technology can be utilised also in the shape of the personal computer, e-mail and the internet.

To support these aspects of personal development, some organisations help their staff to manage their own development by preparing handbooks of ideas and suggestions for possible development activities.

Since this kind of self-managed personal development is still emerging and evolving, you ought not to be just left to your own devices. You may find that you need some initial support and ongoing assistance with the particular expertise which self-development requires. This expertise involves the "enabling skills" of learning. Managers who already possess the skills of their trade (managing), need to add the skills of learning and the skills appropriate to personal development.

Guidance for managers usually concerns itself with the "what" of development. The guidance suggests: arrange some coaching, talk with an expert, undertake a project, and so on. But individuals often need help with the "how" of carrying forward these suggestions.

Self-managed development is very different from trainer-led learning. To undertake it, each self-developer has to be his or her own trainer. Trainers have their own particular skills, expertise and understanding about the learning process; the self-developer has to absorb enough of these accomplishments to ensure that his or her personal development becomes effective. A new world, with its particular skills, has to be explored and understood.

Some of these skills are concerned with setting up a development activity or a learning experience, others are concerned with maximising the learning whilst such an activity is taking place, and yet others involve reviewing the experience after it has occurred.

Taking action

This book shows managers who are pursuing self-managed personal development how they can practise and acquire the "enabling skills" they need, so that they can use work-based learning to its best possible advantage and get the most out of the self-study materials they use.

To help you plan and organise your own self-managed Personal Development Programme and make it effective, use the suggestions for checklists, sheets, forms and planners contained in a special section called THE DEVELOPMENT ORGANISER at the back of the book.

1 Opportunity Knocks!

The Working Revolution

In recent times, we have experienced a revolution in the way that people work – and that revolution is still going on. Attitudes and approaches within the workplace have changed radically, are continuing to change, and will go on changing. Managerial procedures are being modified, managerial practices are being improved and new and different managerial skills are being demanded.

There is now an overwhelming emphasis upon performance, and upon its measurement and quantification. Quality and customer satisfaction are major preoccupations. Responsiveness and flexibility of performance are demanded right across all manufacturing and service sectors. And all the time we hear the words "results, results, results" beating their interminable rhythm.

The Learning Revolution

In parallel with these changes, we are experiencing another revolution – in the way that people learn. Old and rigid notions have been discarded and more flexible and progressive methods are being adopted. This is happening right across the learning spectrum. Nowhere is this change more apparent than in managerial learning.

In the past, working managers in the early part of their careers might undertake management training, usually in the form of short courses. Later they might be the recipients of "management development", perhaps by attending further courses or through some form of wider experience-gathering.

Now we have a much more enlightened approach to employee development, with a range of approaches in use, flexible alternatives available and a great deal of emphasis on PERSONAL DEVELOPMENT.

What is Personal Development?

Personal development means simply the development of the individual person. The term "development" covers the enhancement of existing skills, the acquisition of new ones, the acceptance of new responsibilities, the acquisition of additional confidence and a whole range of processes designed to add breadth, depth and strength to a person's individual capability and competence.

Such personal development can be arranged or organised in different ways and for different purposes. It may be required to benefit the individual in a specific workplace, so that the person can deploy additional skills in that workplace. This process may carry a bonus for the individual, in that he or she enhances their personal CV and becomes a more marketable commodity, either in their existing company or elsewhere.

Alternatively, personal development can be arranged for the near-exclusive benefit of the employing organisation with strict limits on any individual benefit. A third path sees personal development contributing to both parties, with the organisation gaining and the individual becoming enriched at the same time.

In an ideal world, it is the latter kind of personal development which is desirable. In this situation, personal development becomes a partnership between the employing organisation, which has the need and requires the skills, and the individual who supplies their own personal skills to the employing organisation but retains them for outside use and retains the right to utilise them for personal advancement, whether that involves promotion or resignation.

The provision of effective personal development by an employer requires the systematic and comprehensive assessment of individual and corporate needs and then the deployment of a variety of development methods and techniques in order to meet those assessed needs.

What is Self-Managed Personal Development?

Self-managed personal development indicates that the manager has taken responsibility for his or her own learning. It implies also that it is "the self" which is being developed. You'll also come across *self-directed learning* or *self-directed development* and *self-managed learning* and *self-managed development*, all of which are used to cover similar areas of meaning.

All these expressions are symptomatic of the change which has taken place in the philosophy of development. In the past, development was almost always trainer-led and organisationally-directed: now it is recognised that other options can provide the purposeful and effective development which individuals and organisations demand.

We use Self-Managed Personal Development in this book, because it expresses the learning concept more precisely and implies a broader and non-introspective approach. Whilst self-managed developers should take responsibility for their learner-led learning, they cannot develop themselves in isolation. They draw upon all the resources available – peers, bosses, experts, personnel and training specialists, other sections within their own organisation, their partners and their friends.

The Water's Lovely – Why not jump in?

Self-Managed Personal Development is now a proven process. It is effective, it is acceptable and it gets results!

The many different examples of individuals who achieve success through self-managed personal development programmes has encouraged companies and organisations to expand its use dramatically. So if you take it up, you'll be taking up a proven product with a good track record.

The water may be warm and your colleagues may be calling to you, but only you can take the plunge! You have to make the decision! You are the one who has to say: "I'LL DO IT!"

It is not enough, however, to wake up one day and say to yourself: "I think I'll have a go at this personal development stuff." As we've just indicated, it needs a good deal of preparation. To undertake personal development, you need to be committed, dedicated and open-minded.

Taking responsibility for your own learning and managing your own development will involve you in a number of different activities, with which you may be unfamiliar. You will have to:-

- set markers for successful performance
- evaluate performance against those markers
- identify learning needs in the light of performance
- identify learning opportunities
- plan learning against the identified needs
- review the learning processes used

This book has been prepared especially to help you with these unfamiliar processes. With guidance and support, you can join the thousands who are using self-managed personal development with great success. So seize any opportunities that may be offered to you and lobby your boss to provide you with more opportunities to undertake personal development and to manage it yourself.

If you do take the plunge, you'll find that not only can you do your job better, but you feel more relaxed and confident. In addition, your enhanced expertise will make you a much more saleable proposition in the managerial market-place.

So, when you've considered all the angles, say to yourself:

"No more delay, because it's here to stay!"

2 Methods and Approaches

Your Organisation and You

If you are being encouraged to be a "self-managed developer", does that give you free rein to choose and determine the various subjects and topics to be learned? Or does your organisation continue to call the tune, setting the agenda and fixing the topics, with only the method of delivery being altered?

Organisations which are aware of these conflicting demands find a balanced response. They ensure that both individual and corporate learning needs are determined. They stimulate individual learning which will satisfy both the needs of the organisation and the aspirations of individual managers. They build a *developmental partnership* in which both parties have particular responsibilities.

If you and your own employer are both to become involved

in such a developmental partnership, you each need to be clear about your responsibilities and take charge of them. You, for your part, must

- recognise your learning needs
- negotiate ways of meeting them
- seize opportunities for learning
- seek out help, advice and guidance
- create a support network
- review your learning as you go

Your organisation, for its part, must:

- contribute to the recognition of your learning needs
- offer you opportunities for development
- help you with development choices
- ensure time and resources for your developmental activities
- make personal contracts with others, to meet your specific needs
- foster a climate of learning and reflection in the organisation
- encourage experts and specialists to give advice and guidance
- provide scope for you to use your new skills and competences

The Range of Methods and Approaches

A wide range of different methods and approaches is available to help you with your self-managed development. Reading, studying videos, listening to audiotapes, carrying out projects, undertaking short attachments, learning from job-swaps, shadowing another manager, trying role reversal: all these and many more can be used.

The methods available include both the formal and the informal. The learning provision may be either formal and structured or informal and loosely organised. The process used by the individual may have different degrees of formality and structure.

Managers tend to be most familiar with formal courses and learning programmes: these are normally specific customised activities established solely for learning purposes. Such courses and programmes will often be trainer-led, but they might involved a degree of learner independence.

Informal self-development involves the use of activities and experiences which can be adopted for learning purposes. They are often regular, everyday activities which will take place in any case, but which can be given a learning function. The main purpose of these activities is managerial, but they are also developmental.

Work-based self-development means using the on-going work situation and exploiting any ad-hoc learning opportunities which occur. Self-development opportunities can also occur externally, in the 'non-work' environment: many people find that activities undertaken in their leisure and relaxation time are beneficial to their development and can have a learning content.

There can be situations where formal learning materials are used informally by the individual learner. You may buy or borrow a book, but the way in which you use it – in its entirety, partially, reading straight through, or dipping-in –

is strictly a matter for yourself and your own judgement and preference.

Checking out the Best Methods for You

In the DEVELOPMENT ORGANISER at the back of this book you will find a *Learning Methods Checklist*. This lists and classifies the full range of methods which you could choose. Use the checklist to review them in detail and to note the approaches which you think are most suitable and practical for you and for your own self-managed development.

Our Six Development Topics

You, as a practical manager, will be concerned with the specific content of your own personal development. Now management tasks and managerial activities cover a very wide range of subjects and to attempt to refer to them all would be unwieldy and possibly confusing. We have chosen, therefore, six major mainstream managerial topics, which form a framework upon which to set out the various ideas, suggestions and discussions on self-managed personal development contained in this book.

The six topics are listed below, together with the symbol which is shown when reference is made to the topic or when a development illustration for that topic is given:

Teambuilding and Teamworking ¶ *Team*

Leading, Managing and Motivating Lead	¶	*Lead*
Coaching and Mentoring Coach	¶	*Coach*
Planning and Organising Plan	¶	*Plan*
Performance Improvement Performance	¶	*Improve*
Effective Customer Service	¶	*Service*

3 Ideas and Suggestions

Self-Managed Development Activities

Personal development can take very many different forms and personal development programmes can involve a wide range of different approaches. This book cannot provide you with a comprehensive catalogue of all available ways to develop or enhance your managerial competence, but it can and does give you an indication of some simpler and user-friendly approaches.

These simpler approaches carry with them the added and not unimportant benefit of being less costly to undertake. They involve three different areas of self-managed development activity:

- Work-based *development experiences*
- "Solo" *development exercises*

- Using self-study *development materials*

For simplicity, these have been designated as separate areas of activity, but they are closely-linked and the three kinds of experience can be used to reinforce each other. They are areas of activity which you can control and pursue at your own pace.

Work-based Development Experiences

Work-based development involves taking the ordinary managerial working situation and utilising it for learning purposes. The basic nature of the management job remains unaltered, but spaces and opportunities are made to "learn as you manage". The approach encourages managers and their bosses to put a different slant on some issues and to become more creative and proactive.

Day-to-day *working and managing* can prosper alongside *experiencing and learning*. It is surprising how many different kinds of learning opportunity can be carved out and how many sorts of activities and experiences you can make use of.

In pursuing personal development within this area, you should do two things. Informal learning and development can take place anywhere, and at any time, so seize any opportunities for learning which occur naturally within your workplace. In addition, however, you should be as creative as you can and devise activities and experiences which will help to further your development.

Work-based development activities can be used to contribute to the enhancement of every kind of managerial competence. So whether you want to improve your planning, develop your people management, increase your creative skills or organise yourself better, you can use work-based learning to do it. Your theme should be: **Learning at Work!**

To illustrate how your workplace can be used for learning, here are some ideas and suggestions for different kinds of development activities and experiences which you can either arrange yourself or organise in conjunction with your colleagues or your manager.

You will find that some of these suggestions may be appropriate to your circumstances, whilst others may not. So when you try out work-based development, don't just use the examples given here, because they're only provided to get you started.

You'll find it much more exciting and rewarding if you devise your own activities. Do some good creative thinking and work out some activities and experiences which you think will be best for you. You'll get a lot of fun and satisfaction out of kicking ideas around and ending up with something which will help you.

These are our example ideas:

¶ *Team*

Visit a manager who is a good team-leader and who has a well-developed and well-run team. Consult your manager and choose someone in another section whom you do not know personally. When you visit the chosen manager, persuade him or her to provide some coaching on teams and teamworking for you. Discuss team issues. Review your own team actions in retrospect with him or her in order to learn from them.

¶ *Lead*

Make an agreement with your manager for you to "take the lead" in certain meetings or task-group situations. Get some briefing beforehand, review your performance afterwards and seek some honest and constructive feedback on your effectiveness.

¶ *Coach*

Identify a task which you can delegate to a member of your staff, then use a conscious coaching style to help them with the task. Review the coaching process afterwards and seek feedback from the person you have coached.

¶ *Plan*

Arrange to spend a day or two in a section of the company which adopts a process of informed prioritisation, which reviews and adjusts plans on a rolling basis, and which ensures that departmental planning is in line with corporate strategy. Soak up the approach and look for ways to apply what you learn.

¶ *Improve*

Arrange to "shadow" a senior manager who is good with ideas and is noted for initiating improvements. Observe the approach he or she uses and seize every opportunity to discuss change and improvement with the manager concerned.

¶ *Service*

Get your staff together to talk about customer service, in order to improve understanding and involvement. Discuss the service provide at present. Consider any problems. What needs to be done? How should it be done? End by preparing an action plan.

Solo Development Exercises

Solo development exercises are ones which the individual self-developer can undertake alone. They do not require the co-operation of others, or any interaction with other people.

Since your managerial skills and competences involve working with others, you will find that the most helpful development experiences you can have are the ones where other people interact with you and thereby assist your development. Solo development work comes in useful, however, when you want to "get things straight" in your own mind or perhaps practise a particular approach before you put it into effect.

Solo development exercises can be used to contribute to the enhancement of every kind of managerial competence and in the pages which follow you will find some ideas and suggestions given for illustration purposes. Some may be suitable for you, but others may not. When you are ready to try solo development exercises, don't confine yourself to those given here: you'll find it more exciting and rewarding if you devise your own. Do some really creative thinking and work out some exercises which you think will be best for you. You'll get a lot of satisfaction when you produce something which proves helpful to you.

When you have learned something as a result of one of these solo development exercises, don't forget to follow it through so that you can then apply your learning in practical workplace situations.

Here are the examples:

Solo Exercise 1 ¶ *Coach*

Development

Keep a 'critical incident' diary to record, analyse and learn from key experiences during your working day. In our DEVELOPMENT ORGANISER you will find a suggested format for a critical incident diary, which you can adapt and use. Write down in your own words each difficult or significant incident or situation with which you have had to deal. Ask yourself how often you encounter this kind of incident or situation and describe how you reacted to it. Think back over your response and consider how you could have improved the way in which you dealt with the incident or situation.

DEVELOPMENT FOLLOW-UP

When you have reviewed the incident or incidents, write a clear note to yourself about what you recommend. Then plan how you are going to put it into practice. Write that down as an action plan. Then implement it.

Solo Exercise 2 ¶ *Team*

Development

Develop your understanding of team performance by practising your process review skills. Sit in on a meeting, but do not participate in it. As the meeting progresses, make your own notes about what is happening. Use a checklist like this:

- who made the most effective contribution?
- who made the least effective contribution?
- were the purposes of the discussion made clear?
- did people listen to each other? were creative ideas suggested?
- did the meeting help to bridge different interests?
- what were the most helpful actions?
- what were the least helpful actions?
- was the time well used?
- were difficult issues debated thoroughly?
- did the team distinguish properly between facts and opinions?

DEVELOPMENT FOLLOW-UP

Collect your findings and conclusions and use them to report back to the team. Discuss your observations with the team members and plan collectively how you can overcome any problems and improve the effectiveness of your meetings.

Solo Exercise 3 ¶ ***Plan***

Development

- Look back over the past week (or month, or other chosen period).
- Write down anything useful you have learned over that time.
- Which specific activities helped you to learn those things?
- Were there other things you might have learned if you had planned in advance?
- In the light of that, which activities in the coming period offer you opportunities for learning?
- Are you aware of any projects, assignments, committee places, working group co-options, etc., which may come up shortly and which may give you new knowledge and experience?
- Can you put in bids for any of these?

DEVELOPMENT FOLLOW-UP

Put in your bids for the activities which you think would provide you with useful learning opportunities.

Be assertive and persistent to ensure that these opportunities materialise. When you have taken part in the experiences, review them thoroughly, discuss them with your manager and plan how you can apply what you have learned in your daily job.

Solo Exercise 4 ¶ *Improve*

Development

Review your ability to work effectively with other people.

- List the people with whom you spend at least one hour per week - your boss, those senior to your boss, your immediate subordinate, colleagues in your department, people from other departments, customers, suppliers, etc., etc.
- Indicate how often you meet them and for how long.
- Select, from the words below, the description which best fits each meeting:

  dull frank genial ponderous destructive argumentative vague mixed-up workmanlike superficial patchy productive aimless planned formal one-sided frustrating wide-ranging satisfying

- For each meeting, consider the following points: was the purpose of the meeting clear? how did you react to the decisions made? did the meeting produce positive conclusions? were decisions actioned satisfactorily?
- Decide which of the meetings analysed is unsatisfactory at present and consider the changes needed in the way that you work with other people.

DEVELOPMENT FOLLOW-UP

When you have considered the action you think you need to take, discuss this with your Personnel Manager, obtain his or her advice and seek help to make the improvements you are looking for.

Solo Exercise 5 ¶ ***Team***

Development

Check up on how you rate as a teambuilder. Work through the following questionnaire:

(1) During a typical month, do you devote at least two hours of your time to developing a member of your team?

A: rarely B: occasionally C: usually D: I spend more than that time

(2) Do you:
A: plan in advance learning opportunities for members of your team?
B: keep an eye out for situations you can use for team development purposes?
C: leave your team to learn from experiences which come their way naturally
D: consciously create learning situations for team members?

(3) If the performance of a team-member indicates a weakness in an area where you have special expertise, would you:
A: say what they ought to have done and ensure close supervision next time

B: avoid giving them that type of work in the future
C: send them on a course
D: provide another assignment of the same sort, get the team-member to report progress periodically and review and discuss problems as they arise

(4) If a team-member comes and asks about a problem, do you:

A: tell them to come back in a day or two when you've had time to think about it?
B: tell them that it is their job to solve problems
C: tell them what to do
D: ask them what they suggest should be done and how?

Check your score like this:
(1) A: 1 B: 2 C: 3 D: 4 (2) A: 4 B: 2 C: 1 D: 3
(3) A: 3 B: 1 C: 4 D: 2 (4) A: 3 B: 2 C: 1 D: 4

Now rate yourself like this:
0 - 8 You really need to work hard at teambuilding
9 - 12 You are within reach of good teambuilding
13 - 16 You should be sharing your teambuilding skills with others

DEVELOPMENT FOLLOW-UP

Whatever your score, think about how you are going to apply what you have learned about yourself. If you need to work hard at teambuilding, seek advice and put together a mini development plan. If you are within reach, try to identify any small areas which need attention and then deal with those. If you could help to coach other managers, talk to your Personnel Manager and offer to do so. Arrange to equip yourself with suitable coaching skills if necessary.

Using Self-study Development Materials

A great many books, videos and audiotapes are available and suitable for self-study. Such materials are comfortably familiar, readily available and relatively inexpensive. Since the primary purpose of this book is to illustrate how valuable learning can be found and exploited within the immediacy of simple practical managerial situations, our main focus of attention must be upon these traditional learning materials.

You will be aware, however, that developments in information technology have enabled very sophisticated learning packages to become readily available, not only to organisations, but also to individuals. Chapter 9 gives an outline of the emerging possibilities for self-study which these technological advances offer.

Here is a small selection of traditional materials. Get hold of these and study them in your own time and under suitable conditions.

¶ ***Team***

BUILDING THE PERFECT TEAM — Video

By using team role theory, this video shows the viewer how to select and put together the right people to form something approaching an ideal team. Roles are clearly shown as are the weaknesses and strengths of individuals in a team.

¶ *Service*

MANAGING QUALITY CUSTOMER SERVICE Book

A paperback which outlines exactly what managers must do to build a winning customer service team. Delivering quality customer service requires knowledge, skill, effort and the right people properly trained. All the stages needed to achieve this are covered.

¶ *Coach*

COACHING SKILLS Video

Double video covering the concept and skills of coaching. Managers have many responsibilities for the development of their own people, yet many are not equipped with the necessary skills. This video clarifies the responsibilities and shows you how to develop the skills you need.

¶ *Improve*

EFFECTIVE PERFORMANCE APPRAISALS Book

Practical advice on how to make appraisals work for both the manager and the job-holder, including timing, setting targets and structuring the meeting. Questions to ask and the most important do's and dont's are highlighted.

It should be emphasised that the materials indicated have been chosen, not as complete and perfect solutions, but because it is felt that they can make a useful *contribution* to an individual's development.

No single book, tape or video will, by itself, provide you with all you need or want. You will probably have to study several different items, which will perhaps overlap or be only partially applicable. Mix and match to achieve what you want.

In our DEVELOPMENT ORGANISER we have included a list of selected Self-study Materials which provides a good insight into the wide range of learning materials now available. There are of course many others which are not listed and therefore you need to be on the lookout for suitable books, videos, audiotapes or indeed other kinds of learning materials, not least because new titles are being published continuously.

Creating your own Development Activities

The examples, ideas and suggestions for self-managed personal development activities given in this Chapter are all practical, useful and of proven effectiveness. You can take them and use them. They are not, however, learning commandments: please don't use them if they don't fit your own situation or address your own needs. Sometimes you will find that by adjusting and modifying the suggestions and recommendations you can produce activities which are much more relevant to your particular needs. It is vital that you should feel comfortable with any learning activity you are pursuing: if you do not, your development is likely to be diluted.

Alternatively, you may have to devise some entirely fresh, new and different activities to cope with your special needs and circumstances. You must feel completely free to do so. Your needs are unique – they belong to you alone. So you want development ideas which fit your specification.

It's an excellent thing to create your own development ideas, to work out your own plans and to be seen to be independent and self-sufficient. Originality and freshness are highly commendable characteristics. But . . . . . if you come across a good development activity which has been devised by someone else, don't hesitate: use it!

Always be on the lookout for good learning activities. Nose around. Keep your eyes peeled and your ear to the ground. Talk to people who seem to be good at self-managed development, people who have a good track-record. Find out what they do. Don't have any compunction about copying a good idea, if it will help you.

Support and Feedback

As a self-managed learner, beware of becoming too inward-looking. Don't take everything onto your own shoulders, otherwise you'll begin to feel that development is a very lonely business. You need to talk to other people. You need to consult others. You need some help and advice.

Find out what other people think. Get as much information and gather as many opinions as possible. You don't have to take it all on board – you may well get some contradictory advice. Sift what you hear and then make up your own mind.

Focus your thoughts on your own situation and your personal needs. Who are the people you might want to consult and for what reasons? When you have pondered on these matters, jot down the names and the reasons. Include both the people you would want to consult initially and those whom you would want help from on a longer-term basis.

In fact, you'll be putting together a *support network*. The people you select will have to empathise with you and with what you're trying to achieve and they'll need a range of skills, experience and knowledge which can be helpful to you.

Timing

Timeliness and timing are crucial factors in self-managed development programmes. The fact that you have established and agreed an individual development plan does not mean that you are required to be in "development mode" all the time! You will find that appropriate "windows of opportunity" will occur: choosing the right moment to undertake a development activity is essential to ensure effective learning.

Devising your own Activities and Exercises

In order to devise your own activities or solo exercises, you'll normally have to engage in some creative thinking. Creativity is not one of those gifts which nature bestows upon everyone, but creativity training can be provided by specialists or you can acquire suitable creativity techniques by reading and practising. Ask about suitable courses and look through the Self-study Materials in our DEVELOPMENT ORGANISER: there are one or two books listed which should be of help to you.

Your own Work-based Development Experiences

When you have done some creative thinking to devise your own activities, jot down outlines for them. Then use the Work-based Activity Idea Sheet suggested in the DEVELOPMENT ORGANISER to write down the full version.

Your own Solo Development Exercises

When you have done some creative thinking to devise your own exercises, jot down outlines for them. Then use the Solo Exercise Idea Sheet in our DEVELOPMENT ORGANISER to write down the full version.

Your own Self-study Ideas

You may discover books, audiotapes or videos which you feel are relevant to your own area of development, but which are not included in the Self-study Materials list. If and when you find any of these additional materials, use the Self-study Idea Sheet in the DEVELOPMENT ORGANISER to record the details.

4

Making Ideas Work

Putting Ideas into Practice

Let's assume that you have acquired or created a set of ideas for activities and experiences which will assist your personal development. How do you put these into practice? You cannot just sketch out an activity or an experience and expect that it will happen just as you have written it down on paper. You will need to prepare, you might need to practise, and you could need to polish your skills first.

Preparing, practising and polishing are essential ingredients of self-managed personal development. If you don't cover these enabling skills, the development you are seeking will either not happen at all, or will be disappointing, or will fizzle out.

Let us look back at the work-based activity ideas which we have already suggested and consider the questions which arise when such ideas have to be put into practice.

An Example

Consider one of the work-based activity suggestion paragraphs set out in Chapter Three:

> *Visit a manager who is a good team-leader and who has a well-developed and well-run team. For development purposes, it is best to choose someone in another section whom you do not know personally – discuss the possibilities with your own manager. When you visit the chosen manager, persuade him or her to provide some coaching on teams and teamworking for you. Discuss team issues. Review your own team actions in retrospect with him or her in order to learn from them.*

This paragraph illustrates several essential elements of self-managed development:

- identifying what you need to know
- making a good case for development
- contracting with another person who can help you
- reviewing your experiences

Let's look again at that same paragraph and highlight some key phrases:

> *Arrange to* ***visit a manager who is a good team-leader*** *and who has a well-developed and well-run team. For development purposes, it is best to choose someone in another section whom you do not know personally –* ***discuss the possibilities with your own manager****. When you visit the chosen manager,* ***persuade him or her to provide some coaching*** *on teams and teamworking for you. Discuss team issues.* ***Review your own team actions*** *in retrospect with him or her in order to learn from them.*

As you examine the paragraph you can see that even a simple and straightforward activity can raise many questions and possible problems. For example:

Visit a manager who is a good team-leader
How do you identify the manager you want? What sort of person are you looking for? How do you arrange the visit? How do you prepare yourself for the visit? What are the objectives for the visit? How long should it last?

Discuss the possibilities with your own manager
How do you do this? What are you seeking from your manager? How do you make sure that you are both on the same wavelength?

Persuade him or her to provide some coaching
From what you know already, how much persuasion might be needed? How do you achieve this? How good are you at influencing people? What sort of agreement are you seeking?

Review your own team actions
Are you comfortable with review? How will you set about it in this case? Have you got a format for it? Do you need some practice? Will you need to consult others?

These are the sort of questions which will arise as you plan to undertake this particular development activity; they indicate very clearly the kind of *underlying skills* which you will need to have to make the experience a successful one.

The Expertise You Need

Go back and have a look at all the sample activities and suggested experiences set out in Chapter Three. You will see that, as with the example above, each one contains some key phrases which have a similar practical significance. They point to other enabling skills which you will need in order to pursue your development effectively.

If you examine all the examples, together with any ideas which you yourself have written in, you should begin to see that there is a pattern.

In particular, certain kinds of action or activity appear to be needed regularly. That does not mean that the activities are *identical* – they vary according to the context and the setting – but they are of a similar nature. We shall call the activities which are used regularly for development purposes ***core activities.***

In addition, you will notice that certain kinds of skill are needed regularly. You need to be comfortable with these skills in order to pursue your self-development effectively. We shall call these skills ***core skills.***

The Core Activities

A detailed examination of typical activities and experiences suggests ten core activities:

- Identifying and using a "role model"
- Finding and using a mentor
- Using an "expert" to provide particular knowledge or skills
- Finding and using a coach
- Setting up and carrying out a project
- Visiting another section or department to see "best practice"

- Organising an attachment
- Taking part in a working group
- Arranging an external visit
- Following an "audit trail" to trace organisational links

Chapter Five gives more detailed consideration to each of these activities and provides some guidance on how to pursue them.

The Core Skills

We have identified the following ten skills:

- Clarifying issues to your own satisfaction
- Obtaining the support of your own manager
- Persuading other people to help you
- Obtaining information and briefing from others
- Making a "contract" with others about your learning
- Using role play to prepare for activities
- Observing the behaviour of others
- Reviewing your experiences and your performance
- Seeking constructive feedback from others
- Talking problems though with others

Chapter Five gives more detailed consideration to each of these skills and provides some guidance on how to develop them.

5 Self-Development Action

Using this Chapter

This is a reference chapter. Each CORE ACTIVITY and each CORE SKILL is considered and featured on a separate single-sided page. Hints and tips are given which will enable you to expand and develop your approach to the essential activities and to work on the enabling skills that you need.

You will find it useful to consult these pages as you work on your personal development programme. The DEVELOPMENT ORGANISER contains a pre-planner: use it in conjunction with the reference material in this Chapter to assemble a balanced and effective programme.

Ten Core Activities: hints and tips

Ten Core Skills: hints and tips page

Core Activity 1

Identifying and using a "Role-Model"

A role-model is a person whose behaviour and performance in a particular job represent the standards of competence and skill which another individual resolves to emulate. Very often the role-model is selected for a particular aspect of behaviour (chairing a meeting, running a team, choosing staff) rather than for 'whole-job' performance.

The success of this kind of development activity rests critically upon the calibre of the person selected as a role-model. You have to find someone who not only possesses the necessary characteristics for the role, but also shows the necessary readiness to help and assist others.

- Write down a set of selection criteria in terms of standards of behaviour and performance. Then write down another set in terms of willingness, empathy and "user-friendliness"
- Think of people who are known to you and who could meet both sets of criteria
- Seek suggestions from others – your manager, colleagues, and any other staff to help you with the final choice

Your initial visit will be crucial: take care about how you introduce yourself and make sure that you paint a very clear picture of your purpose.

- Plan your introduction by jotting down a few ideas and then thinking through how your conversation might unfold
- Rehearse your introduction with yourself. Find a quiet

corner and go through it – don't worry about talking out loud.

- Think through the questions you want to ask – and the best way to ask them.

In some instances, you could simply observe your role-model's behaviour - you may not actually need to speak to them at all.

Whilst "role-model" is a useful expression for you, it might be counter-productive to use it in conversation with other people. Keep it to yourself!

Core Activity 2

Finding and Using a Mentor

"Mentoring" involves a pairing with a more senior colleague, clear of any line relationship, to provide you with a wise and trusted adviser and guide.

Beware: the term mentor is often used loosely and confusion can be caused by some superficial similarities with both a coach and a role-model. From your viewpoint as a self-developer, the three roles should be distinguished clearly:

coach	person who works with you to develop skills which you have identified
role-model	person whose behaviour and performance represent standards to which you aspire
mentor	person to whom you can turn as a friend and who advises or guides you on your personal learning

A good mentor should be well-respected, respond to individual needs, be a natural 'networker', understand the organisation, be a good listener, encourage and motivate, create trust and have strong reserves of mental energy. He or she needs to be accessible, not frantically busy all the time. A real 'high flier' may not be suitable.

- Discuss a 'specification' for a mentor with your manager
- Sound out other people within the organisation to find someone suitable

Mentor pairs should discuss and agree some ground rules to cover

- Purpose and objectives of mentoring relationship
- Access to mentor and role he or she will play
- Frequency, duration, venue, agenda and recording of meetings
- Links with line manager or other third parties
- Confidentiality of information

Make each mentoring session a positive one. Agree on the aspects of your performance you are trying to develop and focus upon those. Keep a record of your experiences between meetings so that you have specific matters to discuss each time.

Core Activity 3

Using an Expert to Provide Knowledge or Skills

There are times when, for personal development purposes, you need to consult an expert. Often, such an expert will be what may be called a 'technical' expert, involving, for example, finance, information technology, research or engineering. These areas tend to have specialists whose expertise and qualifications are rooted in science, technology or academic disciplines.

Alternatively, you may want to have detailed discussions with a 'functional' expert, involving, for example, marketing, purchasing or public relations. In these areas the expertise stems from experience and seniority within the function.

Your intention to consult these people will usually stem from your need to gain a greater understanding of particular functions and how they operate. This may be either for general background appreciation or perhaps to become better informed about how different functions and departments interface with your own or with one another.

- Sound out your manager, your managerial colleagues, your staff and any other staff about particular experts

When you approach such an expert, be clear about what you want and make sure that the relationship is a purposeful one.

- Remember that you are the "customer" who has sought out the expert as part of a self-development process: you will be asking the questions and setting the learning agenda

- Be aware that your expert may have difficulty in finding the time and space needed for you. Play your part in smoothing the arrangements and ensuring that time is spent constructively
- Explain what you need carefully and clearly. Be aware that two or three short visits may meet the case better than one long one
- A preliminary telephone call can establish terms of reference and help to use the visit time productively

Core Activity 4

Finding and Using a Coach

A good natural coach represents an invaluable asset, but can be difficult to find. Remember that someone who is an excellent performer within their own job does not necessarily make a good coach.

Coaching is not natural for most managers. It conflicts with a managerial style which involves drive, determination and decisiveness. Coach involves being reflective, non-judgemental and non-managerial in approach. A good coach must not, however, just give advice: he or she must also be positive and directive to provide practice, build up experience and secure improvements in skill and competence.

- Take advice from your manager and a training specialist about the qualities you will need to look for. Then establish a specification for the sort of coach you want
- Sound out other people – your managerial colleagues, your staff and any other staff – about potential coaches and scout around the organisation to find someone who fits your specification.

When you've found your coach, you must prepare the ground in advance:

- Discuss your objectives together and reach an agreement about them
- Set some ground rules for your coaching encounters, before any actual coaching begins, and review these rules at intervals
- Use the excellent books and videos on coaching now available to get an idea of how to use a coach effectively

The nature of the relationship between yourself and the person coaching you needs to be defined carefully. Your coach should not "instruct" you and should not behave in any kind of "managerial" fashion.

- Remember that you are the "customer" who has sought to be coached as part of a self-development process: you must therefore be active in setting the learning agenda and controlling the relationship
- Be aware that your coach may have difficulty in finding the time and space needed to coach you. Play your part in smoothing the arrangements and ensuring that time is spent constructively

Core Activity 5

Setting up and Carrying Out a Project

Undertaking projects is a well-established process within many branches of training and development. You need to take particular care, however, when considering projects as self-development activities. The ideal project should have two attributes: it should serve both the business and your personal learning.

- Identify what you want to learn first, then seek out a business-related topic. Ensure that the topic, problem or issue is a "real" one and that the organisation recognises it as such
- Look for a realistic project which will make an impact on the business
- Ensure that the project's sponsor can guarantee that the project is a genuine piece of work in its own right and has clear value as a learning experience. Make sure you set parallel goals for the two parts and review them both regularly.

Since the essence of your self-development is individual learning, you should think carefully about the advisability of any joint project work which may be suggested. It may be unwise to undertake a project with a partner or as part of a small group unless experience of joint working is specifically required.

- Projects which are to be used for self-development purposes are often very different from those which form part of taught courses within a trainer-led framework.
- Discuss any project very carefully before you agree to undertake it, take care that your independence is

safeguarded and make sure that you are always going to be in control

- Ensure that the project brief is clear and is adhered to, that your progress and your learning is reviewed regularly and that the format and timing of that review is agreed in advance
- Discuss and agree in advance the format and timing of the report. If a presentation is to be made, make sure that its terms of reference are clear and that it is to be given to an appropriate audience
- Be aware that many 'subsidiary' learning opportunities occur naturally during a project (planning, organising, report-preparation, making presentations, etc.) and be ready to take them.

Core Activity 6

Visiting Another Section or Department

Visiting another department can provide valuable insights into how other people operate and give you a greater understanding of what "best practice" really means. You need to set up the visit very carefully, however.

- Be clear in your own mind about your own objectives in making the visit. Itemise what you want to learn.

With this sort of development activity, the choice of the actual section or department is very important. You must find the right department – one which will provide you with some real learning, not just an interesting visit.

- Write down your selection criteria for the department and the visit
- Think of sections or departments which are known to you, which could satisfy your criteria and take advice from others about where you should go

When you arrange your visit, you'll need to take care about how you introduce it and you'll have to make sure that you provide a very clear picture of the purpose. You'll need preparation.

- Plan your introduction. Jot down a few ideas in advance and rehearse your introduction so that you're clear about how you intend to do it
- Set things up in advance (who, when, where) and agree a schedule

When you make your visit, you'll need to be well-organised to keep track of what you're seeing and discussing.

- Make careful notes as you go along; don't be embarrassed about doing so and don't rush
- Ask questions
- At the end of the visit, summarise and clarify to make sure you've got everything straight
- Afterwards, evaluate the visit against your objectives and against what you wanted to learn

Core Activity 7

Organising an Attachment

An attachment involves a short period spent in another function, area, section or department. Clearly it has quite a close similarity with "visiting another section or department" and with "setting up and carrying out a project". The preparations you need to make have some similarity with these.

- Write down your selection criteria for the actual attachment in terms of both learning requirements and user-friendliness
- Think of sections or departments which are known to you, which could satisfy your criteria and take advice from others – your manager, your managerial colleagues, your staff, other staff – about where to go

Prior to the attachment, get a clear picture of the purpose and research the information that will be helpful to you.

- Talk on the telephone or make a brief pre-visit. Ensure that a genuine attachment is arranged – not just a cook's tour
- Plan and rehearse your introduction. Write down some terms of reference so that you're clear about what you intend to do.
- Find out if the department wants anything in return. They may have a piece of work which you could do, providing you with a clear purpose for your stay and encouraging them to offer further assistance.
- When the attachment has been agreed, obtain as much information as you can, to prepare you for the

experience. In particular, find out about the people and the personalities who will be involved.

At the end of the attachment, consider it in retrospect and examine it critically.

- Go over everything in your own mind and make notes about it
- Jot down what you have learned from your attachment
- Conduct a detailed review with your manager to determine the extent to which your objectives have been met, and list any practical ideas which you can use in your own managerial role.

Core Activity 8

Taking Part in a Working Group

Many development possibilities and opportunities are provided by working groups, task forces, committees, study assignments and staff meetings. As always with self-development, however, careful preparation is vital if real learning is to take place.

- Discuss the purpose and objectives of the working group with your own manager and satisfy yourself that your participation will have a clear learning value in areas such as teamworking, chairing meetings, communication skills and project management.

When your involvement has been agreed, obtain as much information as you can, so that you can begin to attune yourself mentally to the task ahead.

- Find out about the other members of the group and the personalities involved. If you're joining an existing group, get someone to tell you about what has happened previously within the group

During the period that you are taking part in the work of the group, try to keep abreast of how you're doing - don't wait until it's finished before you look back.

- Carry out one or two interim "reviews" of your performance. Ask yourself some questions, such as: "What happened there?" "Why did that happen?" "What went well?" "What went badly?"
- Use a personal learning log to record the salient features of what happens, concentrating on the process, rather than the content

Get a colleague from within the group to talk things through with you and give you some personal feedback

At the end of the experience, when your involvement with the group is over, consider it as a whole and examine it thoroughly.

Go over everything yourself in your own mind and make notes about the processes followed by the group and its achievements

Jot down what you have learned from your experiences with the group

Conduct a detailed review with your manager to determine the extent to which your objectives have been met

Core Activity 9

Arranging an External Visit

Visiting another organisation can provide valuable insights into how other people operate and can broaden your understanding of good practice. You need to set up the visit very carefully, however.

- Clarify your own objectives in making the visit by talking it through with a colleague or with someone suitable from outside work

The choice of the organisation or site to be visited is crucial. You must find a host company which is willing to provide you with real help and from whom some genuine learning will be gained.

- Write down your selection criteria, including perhaps the main topics of interest, size of organisation, ease of travel and the benefits to them.
- Think of companies and organisations which are known to you and which could satisfy your criteria
- Take advice from others about where you might go – customers and suppliers can be knowledgable and helpful

When you arrange your visit, you'll need to give a careful introduction, making sure that your aims and purposes are properly understood.

- Think through an agenda and agree it in advance, either by telephone or during a preliminary visit. Agree a schedule: who, when, where, etc.

When you make your visit, you'll need to be well-organised

to keep track of what you're seeing and discussing.

- Find out what makes the organisation tick. Look at roles, organisational structures, employee development, communications, etc.
- Make careful notes as you go along; don't be embarrassed about doing so and don't rush yourself into an indecipherable scribble
- At the end of the visit, summarise and clarify with your hosts to make sure you've got all your facts straight
- Ask yourself: "What am I going to do differently as a result of this visit?

Core Activity 10

Following an "Audit-Trail" to Trace Organisational Links

Most organisations comprise various sections, departments and working groups, which often need to transmit documents, materials or information from one to another. Much can be learned about other parts of your own organisation by means of an "audit-trail", a process which involves targeting and tracing a particular document or piece of data.

To set up an audit trail, you must look at your own position in the organisation and at the communication flows which involve yourself.

- Make a list of all the different types, forms and pieces of information which you receive from other sections. Include all the company systems and processes and cover both production and support services.
- Make a list of all the different types, forms and pieces of information which you transmit or send out to other sections

Ask yourself some pertinent questions. If you supply data, what happens to it when it reaches the section which has requested it? What is it used for? Who uses it? Does it stop there or is some or all of it passed on to another section? Which other sections, in addition to your own, supply information to the same requesting section? Why? Map out a flowchart, or perhaps a small family of flowcharts.

- Select three cases, of different kinds, which will give trails which are likely to take you into different parts of your organisation
- Then start to follow the cases. Visit each department along your flowchart and ask them the same questions you have asked yourself. Ask also about the quality of the information they receive from you and how it could be improved. Make notes as you uncover the answers. Build up pictures of the flow and usage of information
- Visit other sections and departments, discuss the trail you are following with them and absorb all relevant information about how they work and their particular place in the organisational scheme of things

Core Skill No 1

Clarifying Issues to Your Own Satisfaction

Self-managed development, which often (somewhat paradoxically) involves enlisting the help of other people, can raise numerous issues and problems. Clarifying these issues for yourself is an essential part of managing your own development.

When you need to do some clarifying, make use of these suggestions:

- Before you discuss a tricky issue with someone else, or ask for specific guidance, go through everything yourself very carefully.
- Use a pencil and paper and jot down all the relevant facts and details. Use drawings, diagrams, cartoons, "mind maps" and any other devices which will help you.
- If you are anxious not to appear muddled about a particular issue, talk it through with your partner or a friend from outside work.
- Nag away at an issue until you feel comfortable with things – your purpose, your objectives, your approach, what you want to achieve.
- If you have a problem which seems to be clear one minute and muddled the next, get someone you know and trust to "interview" you about it. Tell them to be persistent and repetitive, so that you can get things straight.
- Even if an issue seems clear already, talk it through with

someone else to confirm your own conclusions
- When trying to clarify issues, use open questions (which usually begin with *how, what, why, when or where*) not only to other people, but also to yourself.
- Make sure you listen effectively when another person is helping you to clarify a particular issue

Think about a specific issue which is exercising you at present. Take a piece of paper and jot down your own ideas about how it could be clarified.

Core Skill No 2

Obtaining the Support of Your Own Manager

When you ask your own manager for suggestions for development activities, or for role-models, mentors or coaches, don't just take the suggestion on board without discussion.

- Have a full discussion with your manager to ensure that you are both clear about what you want from the experience you are trying to set up
- Quiz your boss about any suggestion he or she makes before you act upon it
- Find out all you can about the person or persons with whom, it is suggested, you make contact
- Use the full range of your interpersonal skills. The book ***Improve Your People Skills*** by Peter Honey (see Bibliography) will be of help to you with this
- In seeking support, make sure that you use the appropriate degree of assertiveness. The book ***Assertiveness at Work*** by Ken and Kate Beck (see Bibliography) will be of help to you with this
- If you want to obtain the full and unequivocal support of your manager, you may need to use your skills of persuading and influencing. Consulting the book ***How To Influence Others at Work*** by Dick McCann and ***How To Manage Your Boss*** (see Bibliography) will be of help to you with this
- To make the strongest possible case for development, and to obtain the maximum support from your manager, focus upon the benefits which will accrue to

the department, or to the team, or even to your manager

- You are the person who knows your own current manager best and is familiar with the relationship involved. In the light of this knowledge, jot down some hints to yourself on the best way to obtain support.
- Check on Core Skill No 3, because there is clear overlap between this skill and that one

Core Skill No 3

Persuading Other People to Help You

When you see another manager to persuade them to help with your development, you might need to draw them out. Are you good at that? Is 'drawing out' a regular part of your job? If it is not, work on the skill and practise it.

- Don't skimp the introductions and the explanations and be prepared to repeat them in different ways to make the impact you need
- Remember that wrong assumptions (on the part of either of you) can ruin your self-development activity or experience, so always explain fully the purpose of any discussion you're about to have
- Be clear about what you want: don't dither or cause confusion. Say what you want and stick to it
- Remember that if you're asking someone else to help you with *your* development, they may not be ready to do so initially. Can you offer any benefits to them? If you can, it will help.
- Search for the right tone needed to get people on your side
- Appeal to the good nature of the other person, seek to get them to say "yes" and stay until they say it
- Agree that all information will be treated in the strictest confidence
- If you want to obtain full commitment from others, you may need to use your skills of persuading and influencing. The book ***How To Influence Others at Work*** by Dick McCann (see Bibliography) will be of help to you with this

- In seeking support, make sure that you use the appropriate degree of assertiveness. The book ***Assertiveness at Work*** by Ken and Kate Beck (see Bibliography) will be of help to you with this
- Think about a particular need you might have to persuade someone to help you. Jot down some hints to yourself to help you achieve it.
- Check on Core Skill No 2, because there is clear overlap between this skill and that one

Core Skill No 4

Obtaining Information and Briefing from Others

For some activities and experiences, you may want to get someone to brief you. For example, if the activity is a meeting which you have to attend, get him or her to tell you about the forthcoming meeting, about the personalities involved, about what has happened previously in such meetings and any other details which are relevant.

- Make sure that you get your briefing from someone who is well- informed and can put everything over clearly
- Make a clear shopping list before the briefing, setting out what you must know and don't be embarrassed to use it during the briefing
- Establish some ground rules for the task, activity or experience. For example: how long should it last, who should be involved, when will feedback be provided, etc.
- Ask your manager to talk about the activity you are taking on and give you some advice on any role and on how to discharge it
- Ask others to give you some hints and tips from their experience, and any useful anecdotes about people whom you might meet
- When you have had a briefing from someone else, you may, on reflection, consider it inadequate, or you may need some additional information. In such circumstances, don't hesitate to go back again and finish the job.

Think about a specific need which you have, for briefing

and information and then about the person or persons to whom you will have to go to obtain this information. Then jot down how you can best obtain this briefing and ask yourself some questions such as:

- What level of authority will I have if I am to deputise for my own manager or for a colleague?
- What critical issues may arise?
- What is the background?
- Who are the key players and what are their views?

Core Skill No 5

Making a Contract with Others about Your Learning

You will probably set up a Learning Contract with your manager to provide a structured framework for your overall development programme and to ensure the proper involvement of other appropriate people. There will, however, be occasions when you will find it helpful to negotiate an informal "contract" with an individual helper as part of your total programme.

- When another manager has agreed to help you, make an outline of what you intend to do together
- A verbal agreement will usually suffice, but sometimes you will need an exchange of memos
- Make sure that your "contract" covers the following:
  the purpose of your collaboration
  the access you will have to the other person
  how often you intend to meet
  where you are to meet
  what you intend to work on together
  how you will review your work together
- When you negotiate an informal contract, use the appropriate interpersonal skills. The book ***Improve Your People Skills*** by Peter Honey (see Bibliography) will be of help to you with this
- To obtain full commitment from others, use your skills of persuading and influencing. The book ***How To Influence Others at Work*** by Dick McCann (see Bibliography) will be of help to you with this
- Think about the kind of informal learning contracts you

may need to establish and the people with whom you may need to establish them. Then jot down some ideas and hints for yourself about how could set up such contracts.

Core Skill No 6

Using Role-Play to Prepare for Activities

Some self-development activities can involve tricky or difficult interactions with other people, for which you need to be well prepared. Role-play can help you to limber up for a particular encounter. In order to use it, you need to enlist the help of another person.

- Think about the most suitable people to help you with your role-play. They must be sympathetic to your needs, willing to help you, have some 'acting' capability and either have some experience of role-play or be comfortable with the concept.
- Share the criteria above with other people – your manager, other senior managers, your colleagues – and take advice from them about the people to ask.
- Choose someone, get them to agree to play the role (or roles) necessary, and to rehearse with you and give you some feedback on your own performance

In playing a role in this way, the person who is helping you should take on the feelings and attitudes associated with the role. This will provide you with a demonstration of what is in store for you.

- Provide the person who is helping you with a role brief. This may be either a verbal outline or it may be necessary to give them a written brief for the role and to discuss it with them.
- Undertake the role-play or the role-plays which you require. Discuss them with your helper immediately and make some notes.

- With your helper, analyse your own performance, consider any remedial action and identify any needs you have for further skill development.
- Practise, with the aid of your helper, the specific skills which have been indicated and try out other ideas which the role-play has suggested.

As an alternative, good preparation can be obtained by asking another person to throw at you all the possible scenarios and potential questions which could arise during the proposed activity. Talking it through in a well-informed and intelligent way can feel less "stagey" than role-play – and can sometimes be more valuable.

Core Skill No 7

Observing the Behaviour of Others

Observing the way that other people behave is a major skill, and an essential one for a wide variety of self-managed development activities and experiences. You will benefit if you can build up your understanding of different behaviours, practise your observation skills and develop greater sensitivity to behavioural signals.

This is a big subject and you may find it helpful to read up about it and to get some coaching from a specialist. There are various introductory books available and you will find the following titles, which are listed in our Bibliography, relevant and useful: ***Improve your people skills*** by Peter Honey; ***Managing People at Work*** by John W Hunt; ***Face to Face Skills*** by Peter Honey; ***Practical Performance Appraisal*** by Valerie and Andrew Stewart

You should tune your observational antennae, so that they take in more information, and give you greater insights into what is going on. Do make sure, however, that your observations are unobtrusive.

In meetings or in connection with other group situations, it is useful to jot down what is happening, so that you have a record to reflect upon afterwards. You need a simple structure which shows where people are located and allows you to indicate behaviour in terms of words, attitude and body language. You can do it in free form on a blank sheet but many people find some kind of format helpful.

Rackham's behaviour categories are extremely useful. He defined behaviours such as proposing, building, supporting, disagreeing, attacking, defending, blocking, being open, testing understanding and summarising. When you are observing people, a sheet with these headings helps you to record behaviour and examine any resultant patterns.

Think about the various situations you might encounter, where improved observation would be beneficial. Then take a piece of paper and jot down some ideas about how you can develop your capacity for observation in these situations and utilise the results more effectively.

Core Skill No 8

Reviewing Your Experiences and Your Performance

The way you review a learning experience will depend upon the nature and format of that experience. Gather informal comments (just a few brief points, no detail) at the end of the activity or experience. Then hold a proper review later with the appropriate people.

- Prepare for the review by jotting down the events in the activity or experience; be factual and unprejudiced
- Review the experience with yourself. How do you rate your own performance, using a scale of 1 to 5? Did you feel comfortable whilst you were undertaking the activity (1 to 5)? What were the positive aspects? Were there any negative aspects?
- Draw out constructive feedback from others. Consult the sheet for Core Skill No 9 to help with this.
- Identify any areas which you need to work on and the skills which are involved.
- Work on the skills as and when you can in your everyday activities.

If you're not very experienced in carrying out such a review, do some homework.

- Take advice on how to carry out a review
- Read up a good text on the subject and make notes to help you when you come to do it. ***Practical Performance Appraisal*** by Valerie and Andrew Stewart (see Bibliogrpahy) is a useful book for this.
- Practise reviewing one or two small activities to get yourself in trim.

Take a piece of paper and jot down your own ideas about what you can do to improve your reviewing capability. Then work on them by carrying out a retrospective review of any activities and experiences with which you are involved.

Core Skill No 9

Seeking Constructive Feedback from Others

If your self-managed development involves meetings or other group situations, ask other managers and participants to give you feedback. If you have been involved in one-to-one interactions, seek feedback from the other party. (This is a more difficult thing to ask, but when you've done it once it will get easier).

The process of giving and receiving feedback is a very important one: it is through this process that you can learn to "see yourself as others see you". Many of us give and receive feedback daily without being aware that we are doing so. You may need to develop a more conscious and structured process.

To be of maximum usefulness, feedback is best given at the earliest opportunity after the behaviour concerned has taken place. Sometimes, however, the potential provider may not be ready to give it immediately or (perhaps more importantly) you may not wish to receive it immediately. In those circumstances, try to minimise any delay.

To help the process, offer feedback-providers some guidelines. When you ask for constructive feedback, suggest some helpful 'rules'. You can, perhaps, say to them:

- Please don't evaluate your reactions, just describe them
- Please don't generalise, be specific about particular incidents
- Think about me as the one on the receiving end

- Confine your feedback to behaviour I can do something about
- Give me the opportunity to *check* what you say, but not to *contest* it

If you can do so, arrange to have a third party present when you are receiving feedback. Such a third party should not participate, but should act as a neutral observer and try to ensure that the feedback-provider is sticking to the rules.

If the feedback from your colleagues points to certain skills or behaviours, examine these if they need to be improved and plan to improve them. Make a conscious effort to develop these in other situations before your next encounter with the same feedback-providers.

If feedback is given in a group situation and relates to a group situation, both the giver and the receiver of the feedback should check out its accuracy with all the others in the group. You need to find out whether what is being said is just one person's impression or whether it is shared by all.

Core Skill No 10

Talking Problems through with Others

Talk to a direct colleague or someone who works with you. Tell them what you propose to do and how you propose to do it and get their comments, reactions and advice. Take on board constructive suggestions.

Before you talk with other people, 'talk with yourself' by doing some preparation. Use a 'preparation sheet'. This need not be anything elaborate: just a sheet with some headings and reminders on it. Jot down the issues and problems you want to discuss.

Use the preparation sheet also to collect your own thoughts together. Get your mind straight and your questions ready. Think through the actions you might be proposing to take, so that you can discuss these effectively with the other person.

If you feel apprehensive about talking to a colleague about your problems, you might need to give yourself some further preparation. Take a sheet of paper and outline three different kinds of problem which you have faced or might face in your managerial job. Then jot down your own ideas about how you would talk through each of these problems with other people. Rehearse your part of the conversation out loud if it helps.

When you go to see the chosen person in order to talk your problem through, make sure that you

- Outline the problem in the way you prepared beforehand

- Don't make assumptions in advance about what they might say
- Block out any personal feelings you have about the person concerned
- Concentrate carefully on what they say
- Check your understanding of what is being said
- Make brief but effective notes to which you can refer afterwards
- Don't think "Well, they would say that, wouldn't they!"
- Spend as little time as possible talking
- Spend as much time as possible listening

6 Building Your Programme

Planning and Organising

When you've got your thoughts and ideas together and have a general grasp of how you want your learning programme to shape up, you need to do some planning. Each programme, whatever its purpose and content, ought to specify:

the learning objectives Make a clear and precise statement about the skills, knowledge and competences which you want to acquire

the activities and experiences Outline the activities and experiences you intend to undertake to attain your specific learning objectives the achievement criteria Summarise the evidence you will seek to indicate that the learning has been effective the resources State the resources you will need in terms of materials, equipment, expert advice, access to fresh experiences and support from others the duration Make estimates of the timescale of the whole programme of learning experiences and indicate the duration of the individual components as necessary

Negotiating Learning Contracts

Your programme will be more structured, purposeful and effective if you "legitimise" it by covering it with a written contract. Such a contract is an agreed statement of commitment and resolve, from both you the learner and your manager, setting out what you will learn and how you will learn it, together with the resources and the support you will need.

Both parties should be clear about what they are binding themselves to do. You are contracting to carry out and complete your development programme, whilst your manager is contracting to give you essential support and provide necessary resources.

The Learning Contract should contain the following:

- the development goals
- the learning objectives
- the activities to be pursued
- the achievement criteria
- the resources to be drawn upon
- the proposed timetable including the review dates

- all the people involved (including other colleagues, not just yourself and your manager) and the responsibilities which they have accepted

Everyone involved should be clear that they are signing a *learning contract*, not simply agreeing to an *activities contract*. This is a very important distinction. The mere completion of a series of listed activities is not your prime purpose – it is your learning and development which matters. You will have fulfilled your contract when your specified development is completed.

You should take responsibility for preparing an initial draft of your Learning Contract and for ensuring that it is negotiated and finalised. Once a Contract has been agreed, you will take responsibility for managing it, for making any arrangements which might be included in it and for organising the reviews.

Once Learning Contracts are arranged and in place, they do not require a great deal of time. Making arrangements for experiences and reviewing learning become second nature and, after the initial occasion, subsequent learning contracts become progressively easier to establish.

Our DEVELOPMENT ORGANISER includes a sample format for a Learning Contract. Use this directly, or adapt it as necessary, to prepare your initial draft.

Using Learning Logs

You will find it very helpful, as part of your self-managed development, to use a Learning Log, which is a structured and disciplined way of recording your learning experiences.

Any learning experience will usually involve the four-stages of the learning cycle:

- having an experience
- reviewing the experience
- drawing conclusions from the experience
- planning the next steps

A Learning Log will help you to carry out the second, third and fourth stages. Think back over the experience and choose the parts which were most significant and important. Make notes, list conclusions, decide on consequential learning points to implement and work out a further action plan.

The following hints can help you make the best use of a Learning Log:

- write up the log as soon as possible after the event
- keep the entries as short as possible
- adopt your own style - it's yours and yours alone
- make regular entries
- don't worry about elegant writing - no one else will read it
- make sure any plans you make are feasible and realistic
- check your log to review what you have learned

The DEVELOPMENT ORGANISER includes a sample format for a Learning Log. Use this directly or modify and adapt it as appropriate.

Reviewing Your Progress

In addition to the regular reviews of your learning that you make within your Learning Log, you will carry out other reviews with your manager at intervals. When you need to do this, you will find that your Learning Log is an invaluable aid.

You will discover that, as you become more experienced in reviewing your progress with your manager, you will begin to have a clearer idea of what you need to record. This in turn will help you to produce a more effective and valuable Learning Log.

Using The Pre-Planner

A good personal development programme cannot be put together in a few minutes. You'll need to do some preparation and some "rough work" first. Jotting down, crossing out, moving things around, adding, discarding – it's likely that you'll have to do all these before you arrive at a plan that satisfies you.

To help you with this process, our DEVELOPMENT ORGANISER contains a Pre-planner. This is a simple sheet which will help you to work out all the aspects of your programme, before you confirm it in its final "neat" version. Your development programme may be either very straightforward or extremely complex or perhaps something in between: in all cases you should find it useful to have a preparation sheet on which to jot down notes.

A Programme Chart

When you have used your pre-planner and are satisfied with the shape of your development programme, you will find it helpful to use a Programme Chart to record it and display it. You can put this on your wall and use peel-off labels to indicate the different activities and experiences within the programme.

Remember that the programme can still be changed and indeed it may have to be changed. Even though you are displaying it on a smart-looking Chart, circumstances may mean that it has to be altered. You can do this very easily, using replacement peel-off labels to indicate the amendments, and your Chart will still look neat. Don't worry if your programme has to be altered several times over: it simply demonstrates that yours is a genuine working programme.

It is much better to have a Programme Chart with several changes, alterations or amendments, representing a programme which is real, practical and achievable, rather than an unblemished Chart which looks impressive on the wall but is not followed through to achieve real learning.

Reviewing Your Progress and Revising Your Plans

When you have made your plans and set out your development programme on your Chart, you will embark on the programme proper, carrying out the various activities and undertaking the different experiences. Whilst pursuing the programme, a number of different things may happen:

you could find that an activity proves very useful, helpful and enjoyable. You may therefore want to extend it or perhaps repeat it or even add a similar activity to a later part of the programme.

you may find that an activity or an experience that you had planned proves to be unsuccessful and unrewarding and you want to shorten it or to discontinue it altogether.

you may find that you have planned an activity or an experience which involves other people and that a key person is suddenly no longer available on the date agreed. In some circumstances, you could work with a substitute person, but it is more probable that you would want to postpone that element of your programme to a later time.

one of your early activities, or perhaps one of the self-study materials you are using, suggests an exciting development experience which you don't have in your programme but feel you ought to have.

a conversation with your manager, a training and development specialist or a colleague, suggests some revision to the programme upon which you have already embarked.

If any of these or other similar circumstances arise, your response should be a simple one. Make the change! Alter your programme! It is your programme, and if any change you want to make is feasible and practical, then you should make it if you possibly can.

Of course, if you do need to revise your plans, you will have to consult your manager, talk to any colleagues who will be affected and then adjust your contractual arrangements if that is necessary.

It is important to have a continuous awareness whilst you are undertaking your programme that it is a flexible one and that you can change it if necessary. Such an awareness helps you to review your activities as they happen and to evaluate their effectiveness. Do try to keep in mind not just the individual activity you are pursuing but the overall programme also.

Sometimes managers can get "locked in" to their development programme to such an extent that they continue to follow it when all the indications are that changes are required. If you think it will help, ask another manager to help you by role-playing "the cynical colleague". If such a role is adopted, you become the person who has to prove that each activity or experience is a positive and useful one: your colleague will always argue from a negative standpoint.

Continuous review, carried out with common sense, coupled with sensible revision will ensure that the practicality and effectiveness of your programme is maximised.

A Sample Programme

So, after all your planning and preparation, what will you actually do in your development programme? To illustrate what it might contain, here is a description of sample programme assembled by an individual manager.

Sally Keen is a Department Manager with a large national organisation. Her company is a progressive one, which operates well-designed and systematic procedures for performance and development management. Her job grade of Department Manager carries an agreed competency profile and Sally's performance and development needs are assessed against that profile.

A system of annual performance contracts is in use and each year Sally, with her manager, draws up a Performance Plan, which is monitored and informally reviewed during the following twelve months. At the end of that period Sally's performance is appraised at a formal Performance Review and then her next Performance Plan is prepared. At the same time, a Development Review is carried out, to consider any developmental implications which have been flagged up by her Performance Review.

At Sally's most recent Development Review, she discussed her performance with her manager and they agreed that three of the competencies in her profile needed some attention. These were Teambuilding and Teamworking, Performance Improvement and Effective Customer Service.

Now Sally is a very good and capable manager, who is very well regarded by her senior managers. So this discussion and agreement with her manager at her Development Review did not mean that she had suddenly become "incompetent" and a liability to her employer. Nor did it mean that she had lost the ability to "deliver" in these three crucial competencies. It meant that certain specific aspects of these three competence areas needed "tuning- up" a little.

In the area of **teambuilding and teamworking**, her manager felt, and Shirley agreed with her, that Sally does not "empower" her departmental team members as fully as she should. The company's policy encourages staff to make decisions and take action without reference to their manager wherever possible and wants its managers to free staff from unnecessary routine checking. Sally is somewhat unwilling to "let go".

The company is looking for continuous improvement in processes and performance, so that **performance improvement** is a vital element in a manager's competency profile. Sally has a good record in this area and has implemented several important changes and process improvements within her sphere of responsibility. These have, however, been changes suggested by others or decreed by top management. What Sally's manager wants to see is more initiative and innovation coming from Sally and her departmental team.

The third competency area highlighted was **effective customer service**. Sally and her manager had looked at the various elements within this and had agreed that, whilst the level of service provided was indeed effective, customer communications needed some attention. Sally, and therefore her department, tended to use verbal communication in situations which called for the greater accuracy and precision of the written memorandum or letter.

These were the development needs which Sally and her manager had identified. Now Sally has put together a self-managed development programme which tackles the needs by using work-based activities and experiences and self-study.

This is her programme:

1. EMPOWERMENT

I understand from both my manager and other department managers that Brian Collier is particularly effective at giving additional responsibilities and empowering his staff. I shall arrange to visit Brian and discuss how he has achieved this, the skills he uses and how he approaches the task. I shall ask for advice and practical hints and tips and then apply what I learn within my own department.

I will set up a "freedom programme" for my department, involving the removal of unnecessary controls and routine checks on individuals. I'll announce that I'm going to try hard to "keep my distance" in future. I'll tell everybody why I am doing it and encourage everyone to respond to it in a positive spirit.

During our regular staff meetings, I shall make sure that I communicate our departmental aims, objectives and targets fully, and give time for discussion. I'll also make a point of highlighting all our achievements. By putting more emphasis on these matters, I hope to encourage everyone to own the performance targets and to recognise their personal responsibilities and accountabilities.

When someone refers a specific problem to me, I will take the time to review, with the person concerned, the process I used to make the decision. I'll check their understanding of this and encourage them to look for a solution themselves, rather than refer to me, when a similar type of problem crops up in the future.

I shall run a "departmental challenge" competition, to encourage all members of my staff to query any procedures which, they feel, hinder the service which we should be giving to our customers, both internal and external. My challenge to them will be to improve our service by modifying the procedure concerned or replacing it with a better one.

How good am I at recognising and rewarding good performance? How do my staff see me? I'll make a point of going round regularly to get specific feedback on this from people in the department. I'll insist on honest and constructive feedback and then I'll act to improve my behaviour if necessary.

I will study the books Empowering People at Work by Nancy Foy and Empowerment: A Practical Guide for Success by Cynthia Scott and Dennis Jaffe. Both these are in our Resource Centre. I'll make some notes as I go through them and collect any ideas which I can apply to my own situation.

I'll borrow and view a video called Even Eagles need a Push, which our Management Development Manager has recommended. Apparently it features someone called David McNally talking about five qualities of empowered people: self-appreciation, vision, purpose, commitment and making a contribution. When I've seen it, I'll probably decide to show it to my staff as well.

I understand that our Resource Centre is hoping to purchase a video called The Empowering Manager and the computer-based training programme Empowerment. When we get them, I'll have a look at them.

2. INITIATIVE AND INNOVATION

I'll set up a mini-project to carry out a retrospective study of a major improvement which was introduced in another department last year. I'll review how the change was introduced and implemented, but in particular I'll find out how the original initiative for the improvement came about and where the impetus for change came from. When I've completed my project I'll have a talk with my manager about it and see how I can apply any insights to my own department.

I 'll go out and talk to our customers, both internal and external, about the service which we provide and seek feedback from them to pinpoint any improvements which they would like to see. Then I'll consult with my staff to plan how we can respond.

I shall take advice from my own manager's manager about a suitable company to visit, then I shall visit it to see how initiatives occur and how changes and improvements are conceived, planned and organised. I shall discuss initiative and innovation with as many suitable people as possible, take notes and then have a discussion with my manager when I come back. Everything useful will be logged for future reference.

I shall badger my manager and others until I get put on one of the divisional process improvement groups which are looking at opportunities for improvement and change. I'll take every chance I get to talk about new initiatives with other managers in the company.

For our team-leader meetings, I'll introduce a permanent agenda item to examine initiatives and process improvement. I'll use that to keep the subject in the forefront of everyone's minds and punch home the message at every available opportunity.

I'll hold a creativity session with all the staff of my department. I'll get hold of some mind teasers and brain stretchers and encourage lateral thinking. I'll arrange for my various teams and work units to be in competition and set problems for one another.

I shall read Effective Change: 20 Ways to Make it Happen by Andrew Leigh and A Manual for Change by Terry Wilson - they're in our Resource Centre. As I study them, I'll make my own checklist of ideas which I can apply to my own situation.

I'll borrow two videos which have been recommended. Managing Creativity (BBC) and Managing Change (Melrose). Both of them could be useful for showing to my team leaders and staff, but I'll decide that when I've seen them myself.

3. CUSTOMER COMMUNICATIONS

I shall spend time with an experienced manager who has established excellent relationships with customers and whose standards of written communication are excellent. My manager has given me a name. I'll discuss the needs and requirements of customers with this other manager and compare experiences. I'll get all the advice and coaching I can and take notes so that I can improve things in my own department.

I know that my own manager is not happy with the written communications I produce. I'll have a talk with her to try to establish what sort of standards she is looking for. Then I'll try and reach those standards when I write a letter to a customer or a memo about a customer. Whenever I can, I'll get her to read and comment on drafts before the communication goes out.

I'll arrange to visit some internal and (if possible) some external customers to get some feedback about our written communications. I'll take a member of my staff with me and we'll assess the impact which our communications have. We'll ask questions about the accuracy, readability and punctuality of our communications. When we return, we'll discuss the results, make a short presentation to our colleagues and decide what we can do to improve.

I shall "twin" with Simon, a department manager whose experience in the company is similar to mine. I'll persuade him to become my "communication partner", so that we can improve our mutual understanding of customer communications and help each other out whenever we need some assistance.

From now on, I shall try something new with every piece of work in which I'm involved: I'll think it through and then mentally attach a "communications guide" to it. I'll be asking myself: "Who ought to know about this?" "What should they know?" "Who should be told first?" "What are the implications of this?" "What are the consequences for customers?" "What are the consequences for my department and my staff?" Then I'll make sure that the answers to my questions produce some action.

I shall arrange to attend the course on Writing Skills which is run by our local College. In addition to direct instruction, it includes tutorials, self-study materials, tutor-marked assignments and a telephone hotline. Before I attend, I'll see my "writing guru" and get him to advise me about what to look for and concentrate on; then when the course is finished, I'll ask him to talk me through what I've learned and help me to apply it within the department.

I shall read The Skills of Communicating, How to Communicate Effectively and Unblocking Organisational Communication and look for help in there. I shall also use The Writing Programme, a video and workbook from Melrose which takes half a day to work through and which I can use at home.

I have heard about an interactive CD programme called Business Words which would be very helpful. It covers all aspects of written materials including letters, memos and reports. Our Resource Centre doesn't have the technology to run this yet, but they are going to arrange for me to visit one of our customers and use the programme there.

Now Sally is all set to embark on her personal development programme over the next few months. Of course, she won't work through it in the order in which it has been written – she'll plan the various activities and experiences to fit in with her availability and that of the fellow managers colleagues who are to help her.

7 Learning About Learning

How We Learn

Many books and articles have discussed how people learn. Such publications can be very complex, very detailed, and cover many different aspects of the subject. Whilst these are of great interest to the academic student, they can lack the precision and practicality which the busy working manager requires.

We aim to paint a simple picture of what is known about learning and about how we learn and we give some useful pointers for use by individual developers.

Many people feel that they learn best from their own experience, rather than through being taught by someone else. Indeed, it is common to hear managers using words and phrases such as: "I've learned by experience!", or "You're always learning something in this job!", or "I learned the hard way!" or (if they belong to the pompous tendency) "I went to the University of Life!"

Those who say such things clearly believe them and there is little doubt that they are true as general propositions. Experience helps us to learn skills, provides us with knowledge and reinforces our expertise. The experienced manager is a better manager than the inexperienced one. The impetus for this book is provided by the idea that workplace experience can offer a great many learning opportunities which will be of developmental benefit to managers.

There is, however, more to it than that. Just giving a person "an experience" does not automatically ensure effective learning. There's an old chestnut about the manager who has twenty years of experience: "that is, the same year repeated twenty times!" Put two young managers through identical experiences and they will not become identical older managers: in all probability one of them will learn more than the other, one will achieve more than the other, one will progress more than the other.

The key to making the best use of experience as a development medium lies in knowing how to learn from experience. Thus effective development demands an understanding of learning and if we are looking for self-managed development, we have to be aware of some basic rules of learning. To undertake self-managed development, one needs to be a self-managed learner.

The Learning Cycle

Learning which is rooted in experience is known as experiential learning. A model of experiential learning, known as the *learning cycle*, provides us with a helpful theory of how learning links with experience and also explains the different individual learning styles and approaches.

The learning cycle was proposed by Kolb and Fry and it indicates that people learn through an integrated process which involves:

1 having an experience
2 collecting data and making observations about that experience
3 analysing the data gathered and the observations made
4 modifying behaviour and choosing new experiences

The theory involves a continuous loop, instead of a linear process. Such a "re-cycling" concept accounts for the phenomenon of repeating an experience, or "experiencing an experience" several times, each time enriching it, and gaining more from it, because of the observations and analysis which have preceded it.

If everyone was equipped with the same fully-functioning learning loop, we would all learn in the same way, with the same degree of efficiency and perhaps at the same pace. As a result, we would no doubt have a more competent and skilful world. The price, however, would be uniformity, conformity and a dull similarity.

Studies have shown, however, that we do not all have fully-functioning learning cycles. Few of us fire on all four learning cylinders in equal measure. Most individual learners favour one of the four "quadrants" and that becomes their preferred learning style. Some like to concentrate on active doing; others enjoy observing and reflecting; some are happiest with concepts and ordered structure; whilst others want to plunge in and learn in an unstructured, ad hoc way.

When you recognise and understand the learning cycle you will have equipped yourself with the following advantages:

- you will understand the concept of a cycle of experiences and processes
- you will recognise that there are different but equally valid approaches to learning
- you will be able to diagnose and understand your own preferred learning style
- you can work to develop the under-used parts of your own learning cycle, thereby strengthening the whole

- you will recognise that you can learn from a all experiences and encounters, not just from activities designed specifically for learning purposes

Learning Styles

The learning cycle provides a framework which characterises the different approaches which people make to their learning. Leaving aside any theoretical model, most people can accept the idea that different people learn most effectively in different ways. In other words, they have different learning styles.

The best known research in this field is by David Kolb, who, having proposed the learning cycle, went on to analyse different learning styles. His definitions provide us with four kinds of learner:

the activist, who learns from concrete experiences and personal activities

the reflector, who learns by observing, reflecting and pondering about events

the theorist, who learns from conceptualisation and from patterns of relationships

the pragmatist, who learns from active experimentation and from 'having a go'

It should be emphasised that no one is a "pure" learner. A person does not necessarily adopt one single form of learning at the expense of the rest, shutting the others out completely: learning can often draw upon some mixture of styles. One form, however, will usually be preferred, because that is the style with which the person feels most comfortable. Instinctive personal preference controls and conditions our learning approaches.

Some people can exhibit a double preference, combining two styles. Through detailed study, Kolb established four statistically valid learning modes:

Converger:	combines theorist and activist
Diverger:	combines activist and reflector
Assimilator:	combines theorist and reflector
Accommodator:	combines activist and pragmatist

The converger is often found in engineering, the diverger in the arts, the assimilator in research and development and the accommodator in jobs with managerial responsibility.

The accommodator's learning style is based on an approach which involves: doing things; carrying out plans and experiments; involving his or herself in new experiences; adapting to specific immediate circumstances; solving problems in an intuitive and trial and error manner.

Do you recognise yourself? Are you an accommodator? Or do you perhaps fit more readily into one of the other categories of learner which have been listed? Your instinct can be a useful pointer, but to find out more about how you really learn best, you will need to test yourself using an accepted diagnostic instrument.

Identifying Your Own Learning Style

A very useful Learning Style Questionnaire has been developed. It is contained in ***The Manual of Learning Styles*** by Peter Honey and Alan Mumford (see Bibliography) and is in widespread use.

You can use this to identify the particular form of learning (or combination of forms of learning) which suit you best. The questionnaire technique involves considering a series of statements about yourself and then marking these statements according to whether you agree or disagree with their applicability to yourself. Why not consult your Management Development Manager or your Personnel Manager about this?

Please be assured, however, that you do not have to complete such a questionnaire - there really is no compulsion! The Learning Style Questionnaire is mentioned in this book because it is an interesting and useful pointer which has helped many people to become more understanding learners. But you don't have to use it: it is not an essential pre-requisite for personal development. You can become a formidable self-managed learner without it.

Broadening Your Learning Scope

If you decide to try it, complete and process the Learning Styles Questionnaire and then plot your own individual learning style profile on a chart. That profile characterises your own learning behaviour. Your profile will be different from those of other people: don't worry, so are your fingerprints!

Once you have identified your own current preferred learning style, however, you should consider trying to broaden your learning portfolio. You can do this by trying out some behaviours which are not so natural to you. Don't worry, it won't threaten your natural style. It will, however, enhance your learning capacity and give you a wider channel through which to pursue your own development.

Here are some suggestions to help with this kind of broadening. Look at the list below and think through how you could use it to widen your own learning scope.

To develop as an *activist:*

- do something you've never done before, at least once a week
- force yourself into the limelight
- practise thinking aloud and on your feet
- deliberately fragment your day by chopping and changing activities frequently

To develop as a *reflector*:

- practise observing others, especially at meetings. Study people's behaviour.
- keep a diary and each evening write an account of what happened during the day
- go back over an event: identify what went well and what could have gone better
- undertake research involving painstaking data-gathering from different sources

To develop as a *theorist*:

- practise spotting inconsistencies and weaknesses in other people's arguments
- analyse a complex situation to pinpoint why it developed the way it did
- collect other people's theories and try to understand the underlying assumptions

- practise structuring situations so that they are orderly

To develop as a *pragmatist*:

- collect techniques and practical ways of doing things that might be useful to you
- in meetings and discussions, concentrate on producing action plans
- make opportunities to try out new techniques, experimenting whenever you can.

The Skills of Managerial Learning

As you become more knowledgable about learning, and understand more about the processes it entails, your skill as a learner will increase. This is a priceless asset in the modern managerial environment.

Today every facet of management and the managerial process is under scrutiny and managers are subject to continuous and unending bombardment. The old certainties have gone: all is change, movement, change, progress, change, adaptation, change, flexibility, change.

To survive in this hothouse atmosphere, you need more than the old skills of managing. In a world which cannot stand still, you need to add the skills of learning. An understanding of the learning cycle, the development of your own learning style and an awareness of your learning skills will be of great benefit to you.

In the past, managers have found that stability is of great assistance in their managerial decision-making. They could draw upon a past experience to help to decide a current course of action, *provided that the circumstances and conditions were comparable*. If they were not, however, they could go badly wrong.

Managers today, therefore, need more than a good memory and an action replay of a past success. The pace of change and the constant presentation of new complexities demands active learning as well as active management.

Your managerial expertise needs to rest upon twin pillars - management skills and learning skills. You need to be able to learn from new experiences quickly and effectively, because there isn't time nowadays to wait for that steady accumulation of experience which a previous generation enjoyed.

When faced with a problem, yesterday's manager would say: "How did I deal with this before?" Faced with one of today's problems, you have to say to yourself: "How can I *learn* to deal with this?"

Your learning skills and your learning management are of paramount importance, therefore: they cannot be just an optional add-on, they have to be an integral part of your managerial armoury.

8 Problems and Difficulties – and How to Overcome Them

Problems You May Encounter

Self-managed personal development can involve particular problems and difficulties, because tackling self-directed learning is not as easy and straightforward as participating in a "turn up and begin" trainer-led course.

On the other hand, the clear and specific advantage of self-managed development is that your learning programme is likely to prove much more effective than the equivalent course. So any problems and difficulties which might be encountered will be worth the extra effort necessary to overcome them. In addition, of course, the process of overcoming difficulties represents a clear learning experience in itself.

Some typical problems which self-managed personal development can bring in its wake are:

(a) poor or incomplete assessment of learning needs
(b) conflicts between your commitment and that of your organisation
(c) unsuitable or impractical ideas
(d) good ideas which fail through poor implementation
(e) unsatisfactory advice and encouragement from your manager
(f) poor timing
(g) programme dilution or loss of learning discipline
(h) conflicts between managing your development and doing your real job
(i) difficulties in monitoring and evaluating your development programme

Tackling and Overcoming the Problems

To help you to tackle and overcome any problems, each of the nine common ones mentioned is considered below.

(a) Poor or incomplete assessment of learning needs
A good self-managed personal development programme must be based solidly upon known and agreed learning needs. A lively and innovative programme of activities and experiences is very stimulating, and could be enjoyed for itself, but if it does not address real needs it will be unsatisfactory and counter-productive.

How you assess and agree your learning needs will depend upon the system in force within your own organisation. Most companies operate a managerial development review process. Make sure that you and your line manager participate purposefully in this process to bring out your needs and to plan any action required.

You will find it a great advantage if your job has been profiled in terms of managerial competencies and your company's management development process is tuned to that concept. In that circumstance you should, in partnership with your line manager:

- review your performance against your agreed job-competencies
- identify any performance areas which are less than fully satisfactory
- consider the reasons for these performance difficulties
- pinpoint the competencies which could have "contributed" to these difficulties and may need attention
- list the competencies which need to be developed further to enhance your performance in the future
- write down your development priorities for the immediate period ahead
- set out your development goals

If you have to hold a "statutory" review meeting with your manager, it is a good idea to use an informal preparation sheet beforehand, to get your own thoughts and development ideas straight and thereby ensure a positive and productive outcome. It is your responsibility to make sure that everything you want to discuss is covered during the meeting, that the learning needs identified are ones which you can accept and that any suggested learning needs which, in your view, are not valid, are properly contested.

Your company or organisation may not have adopted the competency approach, and it may use one of a wide variety of systems for managing performance and reviewing development. In which case, remember that, whatever the actual system in use, you must be equally proactive and positive to ensure that your learning needs are properly discussed, identified and agreed.

(b) Conflicts between your commitment and that of your organisation

Good managerial development will take place if you as an individual are genuinely committed to the learning process. That process, to be effective, will also require the support and commitment of your company or organisation.

If the amount of commitment which you display and the degree of support and commitment provided by the company are out of step, conflicts will arise. On the one hand, your company could be strongly committed to a management development drive but fails to listen to you as an individual and tries to impose programmes which it thinks will be "good for you". Alternatively, you may be strongly committed to an action programme and find that you then get poor support from your employer.

If you are concerned that your organisation is "domineering", here are some things that you should do:

- make it clear at all times that you control your own learning process
- make it clear that you are an equal partner in the development process
- resist attempts to impose a learning programme upon you demonstrate your own commitment by discussing learning and development regularly with other managers and putting forward ideas
- ask your manager: "How can I improve, how can I learn

from my experiences, how can I do things better next time?"
- seek out and get to know other managers who share your enthusiasm and commitment

If you have the feeling that your organisation is "weaker", developmentally, than you are, ask yourself some questions. Does your company

- ensure that management development policy is compatible with and contributes to corporate and strategic objectives?
- invest in development just as it does in research, new product development, new technology and capital equipment?
- foster an atmosphere which encourages the continuous development of individuals, groups, teams and departments?
- provide all managers with real opportunities for development?
- help managers make informed choices about their development?
- agree time and resources for development activities?
- review development needs, plans and programmes systematically?

If you work within an organisation which displays all of the above, then you are fortunate indeed, and you can move ahead with your self-managed personal development in an encouraging and stimulating atmosphere. If some or all of these things do not happen, campaign for them to be instituted. If a progressive environment is claimed, but in reality the company is only paying lip-service to it, then get together with some like-minded colleagues and lobby senior managers to improve the situation.

(c) Unsuitable or impractical ideas

Good self-development utilises activities and experiences. These will tend to give most success if you have plenty of development ideas to choose from. Do make sure, however, that the ideas you produce are tested thoroughly for suitability and practicality before implementation.

As you will appreciate, there is a danger here. An over-concern for the practicalities could stifle creativity and you don't want that to happen. So it is important to separate the process of conceiving the ideas from the process of evaluating them. Use a clear and distinct sequence:

- brainstorm with yourself to let the ideas come freely
- suspend all judgement about the practicality of the ideas
- get all these first thoughts down on paper
- revisit and clarify your ideas and then improve them if you can
- evaluate the ideas by weighing up their strengths and weaknesses
- try to build on any strengths and eliminate any weaknesses before you reject an idea finally
- assess the practicality of the ideas that remain

In assessing ideas, think them through carefully and be self-critical. Ask the advice of fellow-managers if you think they will be able to help. You should think as freely as possible at the beginning of the creative process, then gradually close in with a colder, more practical eye.

(d) Good ideas which fail through poor implementation

You may have developed a very good idea for an activity

or experience which has excellent development potential for you. It is not enough, however, to conceive the idea: you have to implement it, to follow it through and make it work.

Let us take an example:

> *Ask your manager to let you "take the lead" in certain meetings or task group situations. Get some briefing beforehand, review your performance afterwards and seek some honest and constructive feedback on your effectiveness.*

This development activity seems very straightforward. You ask your manager to help, he or she says "yes, of course" and you go forward from there. In practice, it may not prove to be as clear-cut as that. You may have to ask persuasively, you might need to sell the idea, painting a picture of the benefits for you and the rewards for your manager.

- in making the request, choose your time and choose your words with care
- be selective in order to make a start: don't just ask for a blanket agreement
- be assertive about your learning needs, so that you can secure a real and effective opportunity for yourself
- find out about the forthcoming meeting, about the personalities involved, previous occurrences in such meetings and any other relevant details
- agree some ground rules about the meeting processes, so that your manager's role and yours do not become confused or cause difficulties for others
- request advice about the role you are taking on and seek hints and tips based on your manager's own experience

(e) Unsatisfactory advice and encouragement from your manager

If this problem occurs you will need to "manage your manager". Real difficulties can arise if a line manager fails to provide the advice and encouragement you need. It can be difficult to discover or to understand the actual reasons for such a stand-off.

It may be that he or she lacks any genuine interest in personal development or in personal progress. It may be that the "generation gap" is a factor: some managers can feel that, if they themselves never received development when they were more junior managers, together with the encouragement that goes with it, why should they now put themselves about to contribute to the requirements of others?

If such an attitude is in evidence, then the organisation should try to deal with it, by recognising that it exists and trying to combat it by argument and reason. In addition, however, you will have to work hard on a personal level to try to bring your manager on board.

(f) Poor timing

Problems can arise if the timing of a self-development activity or experience is wrong or misplaced. The timing may mean that the experience "fails" or proves to be less effective or rewarding than it otherwise would have been.

Poor timing can happen for a number of reasons: the set date and time could turn out to be inconvenient for you; it could prove to be inconvenient for the individuals who are co-operating with you in the activity; it could be difficult for the organisation itself to provide the proper environment.

Sometimes you may find that the arrangements have all been made and then something unforeseen occurs which conflicts with those arrangements. In those circumstances, it is better to postpone the planned activity until the conditions are more appropriate.

Of course, if you have worked and planned to make some complex arrangements, only to find that there is a last-minute problem of timeliness, there can be a great temptation to persevere, to press ahead regardless. This is usually a mistake. Be realistic. Put off the experience until later, so that you can be sure it will give you full value.

Sometimes poor timing can stem from poor support. If a planned activity suddenly becomes inconvenient, and you suspect a lack of commitment, you will have to put in some further persuasive work on your helpers.

(g) Programme dilution or loss of learning discipline

Programme dilution means that you have planned a set of activities and experiences, but when you actually come to undertake them, some of the things you had planned just don't happen. The programme gets skimped: a three day attachment reduces to two days; the observation you had planned is no longer possible and has to be abandoned; key people are not available and you have to carry on without them.

When you have arranged a complex activity or experience, you cannot expect that it just to happen. You need to put real effort into making it happen at the time. You have to concentrate on your learning from first to last – to keep your learning discipline. Don't let your concentration lapse or lose your shape.

(h) Conflicts between managing your development and doing your real job

You probably feel instinctively that trying to do two jobs at once can be a recipe for disaster – you're likely to end up doing both of them ineffectively or badly. "One job at a time" is a good motto for most of us.

For that reason some people fight shy of self-managed learning: their instinct tells them to keep their learning and their job in two separate compartments. They want to be able to do the job and not think about learning and then do some learning and not think about the job. Going away on a traditional course suits them perfectly.

The message and purpose of this book contradicts that view. Carrying out a job and developing further within that job *can be integrated* and indeed *should be integrated*. Learning and doing can go forward simultaneously, because they are complementary. You *can* carry out a job and learn at the same time. You will recognise that, in many cases, learning can take place whether the learner is making a conscious effort or not. Sometimes, you just can't help learning!

You can, however, enhance your learning, make it happen faster, strengthen and emphasise it, increase its efficiency and greatly improve its effectiveness if you are well-organised, know what you want and set out to manage it properly.

Managing and learning do not have to be mutually exclusive: they should be simply the two sides of a single managerial coin. If you have formulated a logical plan, are clear in your own mind about your purposes and objectives, and are determined to succeed, then you can ensure that you continue to do your job effectively as well as pursuing your development plan effectively. You can also *enjoy* both parts of your managerial life!

The best approach to managing your personal development is to make it just another aspect of management. Manage your learning in the same way that you manage all the other aspects of your work – provided of course that you do those well!

So relax, draw upon all your managerial experience and don't treat self-managed learning as something odd or peculiar. Then you'll find that both your personal development and your management job will benefit and your efforts in both parts of your life will pay real dividends.

By maintaining a focus upon you and upon the uniqueness of your personal development programme, an impression may have been created of the loneliness of the long-distance learner, making your way across hostile, uncharted territory. The reality - your reality - will not be like that.

You should find yourself in a community of other learners and learning activities: fellow self-managed learners, some conventionally-tutored learners, people with individual learning programmes, those following corporate learning programmes, managers using internal learning resources and people using external resources.

Your company should provide a developmental umbrella and give you the individual support you need to pursue your own programme. In addition, however, it will be a great help if you have an awareness of what other individuals are doing and what the company as a whole is out to achieve with its corporate learning programmes.

Always keep yourself up to date with the learning and development scene within your organisation. Find out what other managers are doing and share information about your own learning activities with others. As a dedicated learner, you'll want to feel special, but you don't want to feel isolated.

(i) Difficulties in monitoring and evaluating your development programme

Traditional "trainer-led" development programmes are often monitored from the provider's viewpoint by the programme leader or by an associated training and development specialist. As a participant in such a programme, you would monitor the programme and your own learning from the point of view of a "trainee".

Self-managed personal development programmes, however, present a different situation. You are, in a sense, both trainer and trainee. You have to carry out both varieties of monitoring in order to keep a regular and systematic check on what you're doing and the way in which you're doing it.

First of all, keep your manager in the picture on a day to day basis. Don't flood him or her with detail, but make sure that there is a regular flow of information. If there are any problems or difficulties, discuss them immediately with your manager - don't limp along in the hope that problems will go away.

Secondly, make good use of the regular review meetings which you should have built into your programme. If both your manager and yourself are complying with the terms of your learning contract, then your mutual commitment to these reviews will ensure that they are well-conducted, purposeful and effective.

Thirdly, you can ask a colleague to hold a watching brief and help you by talking you through your programme with you from time to time. He or she needs to just ask some common-sense questions and keep you thinking about your programme and how it is going.

In addition to monitoring your programme, you need to carry out some evaluation. Whilst monitoring means measuring what is happening and keeping a check on the facts, evaluating involves making an assessment based on the facts.

Once again you find yourself on both sides of the provider-user fence. You agreed your own learning needs, you assembled and organised your own personal development programme, you undertook that programme and you managed its completion. You've got the double vision that enables you to see both sides: you want your programme to be a success and you want to succeed as a learner. You're not exactly an independent assessor for evaluation purposes, are you?

So, whilst you should make a contribution to the evaluation of your programme, it would not be appropriate for you to take on the entire responsibility. There are three ways in which it can be done.

Firstly, you can ask an independent person to carry out an evaluation of your programme. This might perhaps be a fellow manager, someone from the same organisation who knows its culture, but has no knowledge of you personally.

In this case you would obtain a totally unbiased and objective picture. The evaluator might, however, miss some essential facts or be unable to put them into context precisely because he or she is a stranger to you.

Secondly, you can invite a colleague whose judgement you trust to carry out an evaluation of your development programme. If, as an integral part of that programme, you are already working with someone who acts as your mentor, then you could ask this colleague to carry out the evaluation. The advantage of this is that the evaluator knows you and knows something about your programme already and can build objectively upon that knowledge.

Thirdly, however, you could ask your mentor to work with you to carry out a joint evaluation of your programme. Although you would participate, your mentor would be the "senior partner" in the evaluation. You can provide the information and the context, whilst your partner can manage the systematic process and provide the necessary objectivity.

Consult your own manager and then agree which of the methods you are going to use. All three methods can provide a full and proper evaluation.

Irrespective of who undertakes it, the evaluation of your personal development programme ought to involve:

an evaluation of the "administrative" aspects of the programme

- Did all the different parts of the planned programme fit together satisfactorily?
- Did the various people who agreed to participate all play their part effectively?
- Were the self-study materials available in the right place

at the right time?
- Were the sections and departments which hosted your visits properly primed?
- Did these sections and departments provide what you wanted?

an evaluation of the effectiveness of the learning programme itself

- Was the overall learning effective?
- Did each part of the programme provide you with what you had planned?
- Were the outcomes in line with what you had envisaged?
- Has your competence been improved as a result of the programme?
- Is your managerial behaviour significantly different now?
- If so, how is it different?

These are examples of the sort of questions which the evaluators of your programme should be asking, but they are suitable for direct use. Since yours is a unique personal development programme, you must sit down with your mentor or your colleague, and together prepare, after consultation with your line manager, in the light of all the circumstances, your own specific set of evaluation questions.

Dealing with Difficulties: Another Form of Development

Please don't be put off by this recital of some potential difficulties. Self-managed personal development is not impossible! We've just taken the precaution of pointing out to you some of problems which could arise. Let us hope that none of them happen to you! If any do occur, however, you are now prepared.

If you do have a problem or two and you have to cope with them, you will find it a very valuable learning experience. Organising and managing any project always throws up some problems: organising and managing your own development is no exception. Dealing with and overcoming such problems helps to enhance, reinforce and consolidate your expertise in a new area.

Once you have set up some development activities and experiences, undertaken them, encountered some problems, solved those problems, completed all the experiences satisfactorily and evaluated those experiences, you will be in possession of some sound expertise in self-managed personal development. If you regard any organisational problems as part of your learning experience, the satisfaction you feel in dealing with them will be all the greater.

To be effective and rewarding, self-managed personal development has to well- prepared and well organised: that's why this book provides you with detailed guidance on how to tackle it and that's why it covers all the different aspects. If you're systematic and purposeful in your approach and you use ordinary common sense, then self-managed development is very, very, straightforward.

So be positive, keep a clear check on what you're doing, enlist the help of your colleagues, make sure that your manager fulfils his or her contract and go for it!

9 Using Technology in your Personal Learning

The Simple or the Sophisticated?

Self-managed personal development, as envisaged within this book, should involve you as a manager in utilising available learning opportunities within your workplace and in pursuing self-study using books, audiotapes and videos. To encourage you to begin, and to keep you going when you have begun, our deliberate emphasis throughout has been upon the use of simple, easily-arranged and minimum-cost approaches.

Once you have determined your own learning needs, you can arrange one or two activities and experiences, sort out the details informally with your colleagues and then go ahead and learn without further ado. You can change the arrangements, spend longer or shorter times than first envisaged, or make any other alterations, if you so wish. The simplicity and the informality give you valuable flexibility.

If you want to support these experiences with some self-study, you can borrow a relevant book or perhaps buy it (if it is in paperback) and go ahead and read it (probably at home) and make some notes on it. In addition, you might want to listen to an appropriate audiotape in your car. In principle, you can do this whether you are engaged on business or pleasure, but in practice the views of any other occupants of the car may have to be taken into account. Your further form of self-study is of course the video, which you can borrow and slip into your video recorder at an appropriate time, usually when you are alone!

In all these cases, you do not need to read, listen or view continuously - you can dip into sections, skip back and forth and stop and start when feel you should. You are in complete control of your learning.

The use of electronic technology is now an everyday part of our lives. The vast majority of people nowadays own audiotape players and video players and the use of these for learning purposes is a completely straightforward matter. The Personal Computer is now standard issue in most businesses and in many homes and it has much to offer as a facilitator of self-managed personal development. This extended role for the Personal Computer in relation to individual learning stems from two major developments.

In the first place, the PC has expanded from a limited but helpful device used for carrying out word-processing, mailings, accounting and other mundane tasks into an exciting "window on the world", capable of gathering information and news, tracking data and networking with other individuals having similar interests. Secondly, the advent of advanced processors has enabled the PC to go "multi-media" and to play CD-Rom learning packages which combine text, sound, still pictures and video.

Once you are equipped with all the relevant and up-to-the-minute technology, you can explore four potential "personal development" applications of your PC:

A Using online services to research factual information about published learning materials and resources and to investigate their availability

B Using appropriate online services to locate suitable materials and to download these ready for individual personal study

C Using appropriate online services to create and build coaching links with suitable individuals or to establish peer partnerships for mutually-beneficial learning

D Using multimedia learning packages for self-study at a time of your own choosing and at your own pace in parallel with your use of simpler materials such as books or tapes

The technological revolution which has brought these possibilities is still proceeding - and at such a pace that it is dangerous indeed to attempt descriptions which may be out of date before this book is published. The purpose of this short chapter, therefore, is merely to flag up the possibilities which are now emerging and then to urge you to investigate further so that you can consider adding these more sophisticated learning approaches to the simpler ones you may already be using if you so wish.

Gathering Information about Materials and Resources

Commercial computer online services and local bulletin boards, together with the Internet, all transmit information to a PC via a telephone line and a modem. Both online services and bulletin boards are usually networked to increase membership and content, but bulletin board systems are generally more limited in what they offer.

Online services can provide access to information, advice, reference materials, library catalogues and specialised databases. Choosing the right online service can be difficult and you need to make sure that you subscribe to one that will provide the type of continuously-updated information about human resource development that you want.

The Internet is a global collection of separate and diverse educational, public organisation and private systems. It is not a commercial information service as such, but is open to all computer users and gives access to unimaginable stocks of information. Most commercial online providers offer access to the Internet as well, but Internet-only providers are cheaper and more satisfactory if that is all you want.

Whilst the Internet is by far the largest and most comprehensive of the information services available, it is much harder to access and navigate. This is because it embraces a very diverse number of computer types and operating systems, all attempting to communicate using a common language. In addition, users find that they have to wade through a great deal of irrelevant material to find what they want, whereas online services organise and package their information and provide a certain amount of editorial guidance.

Most users find it essential that their online provider offers full access to electronic mail services, to file transfer services, to the accessing of programmes and applications, and to appropriate conferencing services.

If you subscribe to an online service, this could enhance your self-managed personal development programme by enabling you to seek out new information about relevant learning resources. At the same time, you should recall the old saying about sledgehammers and nuts: your old-style paper-based resource lists may remain adequate and continue to serve you well. So it may not be worthwhile to invest in expensive equipment and services for such a relatively limited purpose. On the other hand, if you already have a system in place, you might as well try extending its use.

Accessing Materials for Self-Study

Online services can give you access to the data-bases of various organisations which allow you to see up-to-date listings of books in print, categorised summaries of resources which cover particular subject areas and short descriptions of new resources.

In some instances also, there may be the opportunity to access actual material in the form of helpful articles or other types of textual material which you can scan, select, download and use. Whilst it is helpful to use technology to acquire information about where to find materials, there is much more value and immediacy in being able to access and use resources directly via your own computer.

At present, online services are good at handling text and simple graphics, but cannot cope with photographs, sound and video. Improvements in modems, the development of compression technology and the provision of local cable networks should, however, soon lead to the full range of multimedia facilities becoming available online.

When that stage is reached, customers will be able, by paying online, to download multimedia software directly into their PC. Such a prospect has very considerable implications for individual learning and for self-managed personal development.

Using Electronic Links to Pursue Personal Learning

Discussions with colleagues are an integral part of the personal development process. The technology is available to enable you to have discussions with colleagues or other managers who are interested in mutual development programmes. You can send and receive e-mail, you can use conferencing facilities or you can seek answers to problems by advertising those problems on local bulletin boards. The use of such methods for self-managed personal development is in its infancy, but it is likely to have an increasing part to play.

You should note the word "part", however, because it seems very unlikely that such contacts will replace the personal face-to-face discussion. The personal computer and its online services do not, as yet, replicate the living dynamic of the old-fashioned chat. Whilst it is now possible to see the other person or persons on a screen, to hear what they say, to note the tone of their voice when they say it, to observe their body language, and to have a verbatim record of the exchanges, there is still a residual "glass partition" effect. Genuine eye-contact cannot be replicated, warmth, interest and enthusiasm do not readily cross the screen and a genuine (and genuinely helpful) conversation may be only partially achieved.

Using Multimedia Learning Packages

The use of multimedia learning packages for individual managerial learning is still at the pioneering stage. The makers have concentrated initially upon the children's market in order to provide edutainment – titles which mix education and entertainment and make learning fun for children.

Multimedia is challenging the traditional ways of conveying information, however, and its potential for genuine "lifelong learning" applications for mature adults could be huge. Keep a close eye on developments and explore some children's packages and some all-age encyclopedias in order to assess the possibilities for yourself.

Sorry, but it's your Decision Again!

If you are to pursue self-managed personal development, you will have to make some decisions about the kind of resources and learning materials you want to use. If you are a newcomer to personal development, you might be better advised to stick to the easily-accessible books, audiotapes and videos. If you own or have access to a suitable computer with appropriate power, you could have a look at what it can make available to you now. If you're thinking of investing in the technology for your family, you might as well do so and then take the opportunity to study the implications for serious personal learning.

We urge you to gather all the accurate information available, to explore as widely but as inexpensively as you can and then to try not to invest in a product a few days before it becomes obsolete. Above all, don't make the mistake of thinking that a product or a process is automatically of greater value for learning purposes if it comes to you electronically.

You should beware of multimedia titles which turn out to be no better (or even a good deal worse) than a book. Books have been around for a very long time. They've could just have something to teach us for a little while longer.

If you do reach out for the wonderful helping hand that technology has provided us with, so please remember that you should not discard the older and simpler approaches. The answer to our question: "Simple or sophisticated?" should always be: "Simple AND sophisticated"

Bibliography

ASSERTIVENESS AT WORK
Ken and Kate Back
McGraw-Hill

CAREER DEVELOPMENT AND PLANNING
Malcolm Peel
McGraw-Hill

DEVELOP YOUR MANAGEMENT POTENTIAL
Charlotte Chambers et al
Kogan Page

FACE TO FACE SKILLS
Peter Honey
Gower

HOW TO INFLUENCE OTHERS AT WORK
Dick McCann

Butterworth-Heinemann
LEARN HOW TO STUDY
Derek Rowntree
Warner

HOW TO STUDY EFFECTIVELY
Freeman and Meed
Collins Educational

IMPROVE YOUR PEOPLE SKILLS
Peter Honey
Institute of Personnel and Development

MANAGING PEOPLE AT WORK
John W Hunt
McGraw-Hill

PRACTICAL PERFORMANCE APPRAISAL
Valerie and Andrew Stewart
Gower

RESOURCE-BASED LEARNING
Julie Dorrell
McGraw-Hill

TEACH YOURSELF WITH OPEN LEARNING
Derek Rowntree
Kogan Page

THE MANUAL OF LEARNING STYLES
Peter Honey and Alan Mumford
Honey

THE OPPORTUNIST LEARNER
Peter Honey and Alan Mumford
Honey

THE MANUAL OF LEARNING OPPORTUNITIES
Peter Honey and Alan Mumford
Honey

THE UNBLOCKED MANAGER
Mike Woodcock and Dave Francis
Gower

USING YOUR LEARNING STYLES
Peter Honey and Alan Mumford
Honey

HOW TO MANAGE YOUR LEARNING ENVIRONMENT
Peter Honey and Alan Mumford
Honey

HOW TO MANAGE YOUR BOSS
Christie Kennard
Gower

The Development Organiser

1. Learning Methods Checklist
2. Critical Incident Diary Sheet
3. Work-Based Activity Data Sheet
4. Solo Exercise Idea Sheet
5. Self-Study Idea Sheet
6. Pre-Planner
7. Learning Contract Format
8. Learning Log Format
9. Self-Study Materials
   Teambuilding and Teamworking
   Leading, Managing and Motivating
   Coaching and Mentoring
   Planning and Organising
   Performance Improvement
   Effective Customer Service

1. Learning Methods Checklist

Your Checks

CHECK A (Desirable): Your own personal preferred learning methods

CHECK B (Practical): Methods offered by your organisation, or for which facilities could be made available by your organisation

CHECK C (Actual): Final choice of methods for your own specific programme

	Learning Method	**Check A**	**Check B**	**Check C**
	Work-Based Activities			
1	Undertake a project			
2	Visit other departments			
3	Go on an attachment to another section			
4	Swap jobs with another manager			
5	Exchange roles in meetings			
6	Deputise for your manager			
7	Follow an audit trail			
8	Be seconded to another department			
9	Use role play to prepare for activities			
10	Serve on a working group			
11	Organise a team seminar			
12	Participate in a business simulation			
13	Shadow another manager			
14	"Network" with other managers			
15	Be coached by your manager			

Learning Method	Check A	Check B	Check C
16 Be guided by a mentor			
17 Twin with a colleague for mutual guidance			
18 Take on added or delegated responsibilities			
19 Take part in an action learning set			
20 Carry out a survey and write a report			
External Activities			
21 Be active in your professional body			
22 Work on schools-industry linkages			
23 Take office in community club, society or group			
24 "Network" with external managers			
25 Go on an attachment to another organisation			
Self-Study			
26 Borrow and use books and learning packs			
27 Listen to audiotapes			
28 Borrow, view and study videos			
29 Use libraries and information departments			
30 Undertake an open learning programme			
31 Study for a professional qualification			
Technology-Based Learning			
32 Use interactive video			
33 Use computer-based training			

Learning Method	Check A	Check B	Check C
34 Use CD-Rom packages			
Tutor-Led Learning			
35 Participate in courses			
36 Participate in development workshops			
37 Attend conferences			
38 Take part in unfamilar training (eg outdoors)			
Represent Your Organisation			
39 Act as a staff representative			
40 Be a representative on a board or committee			
41 Act as host/guide to company visitors			
Develop Others			
42 Coach your own staff			
43 Speak on training courses			
44 Delegate part of your job			

2. Critical Incident Diary Sheet

Date	Description of incident or occurence	Comments	Implications and/or proposed action

3. Work-Based Activity Idea Sheet

Description of proposed activity			Outcome
Who else involved?	Resource/cost implications?	Timescale?	Permission needed?

4. Solo Exercise Idea Sheet

Description of proposed exercise	Purpose

Any cost implications?	Timescale?	Permission needed?

5. Self-Study Idea Sheet

Proposed self-study materials	Purpose

Cost and availability?	How are materials used?	Details for purchase/hire?	Approval required?

6. Pre-Planner

Competences/topics/subjects I need to tackle	Learning methods I will use
Activities I will undertake	My Manager's role and involvement
	Other people from whom I need help
	Time-scale of my programme
	Monitoring and reviewing my programme

7. Learning Contract

Made between .... (learner) AND .... (manager)
AND ....
AND ....
AND ....

Learning Objectives
Outline of activities and experiences
Achievement criteria
Resources
Duration of contract

Date .... Signed .... Signed ....

Signed .... Signed ....

8. Learning Log

(Use this during the period of your whole programme, not just during a planned activity)

Date	Activity experience	Today's important learning points	Further action needed

9. Self-Study Materials

Teambuilding and Teamworking

BRIEF ENCOUNTERS, (Video), Melrose [ ]

BUILDING THE PERFECT TEAM, (Video), Video Arts [ ]

COACHING THE TEAM, (Video), BBC Training Videos [ ]

CREATING TEAMWORK, (Audiotape), Careertrack [ ]

EFFECTIVE TEAM BUILDING, (Book), John Adair, Gower [ ]

MAKING MEETINGS WORK, (Book), Alan Barker, The Industrial Society [ ]

MANAGEMENT TEAMS: WHY THEY SUCCEED OR FAIL, (Book), Meredith Belbin, Butterworth-Heinemann [ ]

MOTIVATING THE TEAM, (Video), Melrose [ ]

SUCCESSFUL TEAM BUILDING, (Book), John Davis et al, Kogan Page [ ]

SUPERTEAMS: A BLUEPRINT FOR ORGANISATIONAL SUCCESS, (Book), Colin Hastings, Fontana-Collins [ ]

TALKING TO THE TEAM: HOW TO RUN A MEETING, (Video), Video Arts [ ]

TEAM BUILDING: AN EXERCISE IN LEADERSHIP, (Book), Robert B Maddux, Kogan Page [ ]

TEAM BUILDING – A QUESTION OF BALANCE, (Video), Fenman Training [ ]

TEAM ROLES AT WORK, (Book), Meredith Belbin, Butterworth-Heinemann [ ]

TEAM DEVELOPMENT MANUAL, (Book), Mike Woodcock, Gower [ ]

TEAM BUILDING, (Audiotape), Careertrack [ ]

TEAMBUILDING, (Book), Alastair Frazer and Suzanne Neville, The Industrial Society [ ]

TEAMS AND LEADERS, (Video), Melrose [ ]

THE TEAM SOLUTION, (Video), BBC Training Videos [ ]

THE ONE-MINUTE MANAGER BUILDS HIGH-PERFORMANCE TEAMS, (Book), Blanchard et al, Fontana [ ]

BUILD A GREAT TEAM, (Book), Ros Jay, Pitman [ ]

HOW TO LEAD A WINNING TEAM, (Book), Morris, Willcocks and Knasel, Pitman [ ]

SUCCESS THROUGH TEAMWORK, (Book), Richard Chang, Kogan Page [ ]

THE DYNAMICS OF TEAMS, (Video), BBC for Business [ ]

Leading, Managing and Motivating

ACTION-CENTRED LEADER, (Book), John Adair, The Industrial Society [ ]

ASSERTIVENESS AT WORK, (Book), Ken and Kate Back, McGraw-Hill [ ]

BECOMING A DIFFERENCE MAKER, (Audiotapes), Flex Training [ ]

CASE STUDIES IN LEADERSHIP, (Video), Video Arts [ ]

DEALING WITH DIFFICULT PEOPLE, (Book), Roberta Cava, Piatkus Books [ ]

DELEGATING FOR RESULTS, (Book), Robert B Maddux, Kogan Page [ ]

EMPOWERING PEOPLE AT WORK, (Book), Nancy Foy, Gower [ ]

EMPOWERMENT: BUILDING A COMMITTED WORKFORCE, (Book), Scott and Jaffe, Kogan Page [ ]

ENABLING LEADERSHIP, (Book), Tom Jaap and Sheila Hampshire, Gower [ ]

EVEN EAGLES NEED A PUSH, (Video), Melrose [ ]

FEEDBACK TECHNIQUES, (Video), Fenman Training [ ]

FIFTY ACTIVITIES FOR DEVELOPING MANAGEMENT SKILLS: VOL 8, (Book), Clifford Johnson, Gower [ ]

HIGH IMPACT LEADERSHIP, (Video), Flex Training [ ]

HOW TO MANAGE YOUR BOSS, (Book), Christie Kennard, Gower [ ]

HOW TO DELEGATE WORK AND ENSURE ITS DONE RIGHT, (Audiotape), Careertrack [ ]

HOW TO MOTIVATE PEOPLE, (Audiotape), Motivation Cassettes [ ]

HOW TO INFLUENCE OTHERS AT WORK, (Book), Dick McCann, Butterworth-Heinemann [ ]

HOW TO BE AN EVEN BETTER MANAGER, (Book), Michael Armstrong, Kogan Page [ ]

IMPROVE YOUR PEOPLE SKILLS, (Book), Peter Honey, Institute of Personnel and Development [ ]

LEADERSHIP AND THE ONE-MINUTE MANAGER, (Video), Melrose [ ]

MANAGING PEOPLE AT WORK, (Book), John W Hunt, McGraw-Hill [ ]

MANAGING ACTIVITIES AND RESOURCES, (Book), Roger Bennett, Kogan Page [ ]

MANAGING PERFORMANCE, (Video), BBC Training Videos [ ]

MANAGING BY WANDERING AROUND, (Video), Melrose [ ]

MOTIVATIONAL LEADERSHIP, (Book), Alfred Tack, Gower [ ]

ON BECOMING A LEADER, (Book), Warren Bennis, Business Books [ ]

ON BECOMING A LEADER, (Audiotapes), Flex Training [ ]

SEE FOR YOURSELF - A MANAGER'S GUIDE TO WALKING THE JOB, (Video), The Industrial Society [ ]

SITUATIONAL LEADERSHIP, (Audiotapes), Flex Training [ ]

SOLVING PEOPLE PROBLEMS, (Book), Peter Honey, McGraw-Hill [ ]

STYLES OF LEADERSHIP, (Video), Longman [ ]

THE EMPOWERING APPRAISAL, (Video),
BBC Training Videos [ ]

THE EMPOWERING MANAGER, (Video), Melrose [ ]

THE GOAL: A PROCESS OF ONGOING IMPROVEMENT, (Book),
Eliyahu Goldratt and Jeff Cox, Gower [ ]

THE GODS OF MANAGEMENT, (Video), Melrose Masterclasses [ ]

THE LEADERSHIP CHALLENGE, (Videos),
BBC for Business [ ]

THE ONE-MINUTE MANAGER, (Book),
Ken Blanchard and Spencer Johnson, Fontana [ ]

HIGH-IMPACT LEADERSHIP, (Video), Careertrack [ ]

LEADERSHIP, (Video), Creative Management [ ]

BUSINESS LEADERSHIP, (Book), V J Shackleton, Routledge [ ]

MANAGERIAL LEADERSHIP, (Book), Peter L Wright, Routledge [ ]

STRATEGY AND LEADERSHIP, (Book), Brian Leavey and David Wilson, Routledge [ ]

MOTIVATING PEOPLE IN TODAY'S WORKPLACE, (Audiotape or Video), Careertrack [ ]

Coaching and Mentoring

COACHING SKILLS, (Video), Fenman Training [ ]

COACHING FOR RESULTS, (Video), BBC Training Videos [ ]

COACHING SKILLS, (Video), Fenman Training [ ]

COACHING SKILLS, (CBT), Maxim Training [ ]

COACHING FOR PERFORMANCE, (Book), Sir John Whitmore, Brealey Publishing [ ]

EVERYONE NEEDS A MENTOR, (Book), David Clutterbuck, Institute of Personnel and Development [ ]

FACE TO FACE SKILLS, (Book), Peter Honey, Gower [ ]

HELPING PEOPLE LEARN: THE MANAGER'S ROLE, (Video), Melrose [ ]

HOW MANAGERS DEVELOP MANAGERS, (Book), Alan Mumford, Gower [ ]

THE MANUAL OF LEARNING OPPORTUNITIES, (Book), Peter Honey and Alan Mumford, Honey [ ]

THE MANUAL OF LEARNING STYLES, (Book), Peter Honey and Alan Mumford, Honey [ ]

THE LINE MANAGER AS DEVELOPER, (Learning Pack), Henley Distance Learning [ ]

THE MANAGER AS COACH, (Video), Flex Training [ ]

THE COACH, (Video), Melrose [ ]

THE MANAGER AS COACH AND MENTOR, (Book), Eric Parsloe, Institute of Personnel and Development [ ]

PRACTICAL COACHING SKILLS FOR MANAGERS, (Audiotape or Video), Careertrack [ ]

COACHING AND MENTORING, (Book), Nigel MacLennon, Gower [ ]

COACHING THROUGH EFFECTIVE FEEDBACK, (Book), Paul J Jerome, Kogan Page [ ]

MENTORING IN ACTION, (Book), David Megginson and David Clutterbuck, Kogan Page [ ]

SUCCESSFUL MENTORING IN A WEEK, (Book), Stephen Carter and Gareth Lewis, Headway [ ]

COACHING, MENTORING AND ASSESSING, (Book), Eric Parsloe, Kogan Page [ ]

Planning and Organising

A SYSTEMATIC APPROACH TO GETTING RESULTS, (Book), Surya Lovejoy, Gower [ ]

A PERFECTLY NORMAL DAY, (Video), Connaught Training [ ]

A PROJECT MANAGER'S HANDBOOK, (Book), Graham Lashbrooke, Kogan Page [ ]

HAVE PROJECT WILL MANAGE, (Video), BBC Training Videos [ ]

PUTTING THE ONE-MINUTE MANAGER TO WORK, (Book), Ken Blanchard and Robert Lorber, Fontana [ ]

SETTING OBJECTIVES, (Video), Fenman Training [ ]

STRATEGIC PLANNING WORKBOOK, (Book), Karsten G Hellebust and Joseph C Krallinger, John Wiley [ ]

STRATEGIC PLANNING, (Book), George A Steiner, Collier Macmillan [ ]

TARGET SETTING, (Book), Ian Lawson,
The Industrial Society [ ]

THE UNORGANISED MANAGER, (Video), Video Arts[ ]

THE ORGANISED EXECUTIVE, (Book), Stephanie
Winston, Kogan Page [ ]

THE ORGANISED EXECUTIVE, (Audiotape),
Nightingale-Conant [ ]

THE OUTPUT-ORIENTED MANAGER, (Book),
Bill Reddin, Gower [ ]

A PRACTICAL GUIDE TO PROJECT PLANNING,
(Book), Celia Burton and Norma Michael, Kogan Page [ ]

Performance Improvement

A MANUAL FOR CHANGE, (Book), Terry Wilson,
Gower [ ]

ACHIEVING CHANGE: A SYSTEMATIC APPROACH,
(Book), Tom Lupton and Ian Tanner, Gower [ ]

APPRAISING YOUR STAFF, (Book), Philip Moon,
Kogan Page [ ]

CREATIVE THINKING TECHNIQUES, (CBT),
Maxim Training [ ]

EFFECTIVE PERFORMANCE MANAGEMENT, (Book),
John Lockett, Kogan Page [ ]

EFFECTIVE PERFORMANCE APPRAISALS, (Book),
Robert B Maddux, Kogan Page [ ]

IMPROVING EMPLOYEE PERFORMANCE, (Book),
Herman E Zaccarelli, Kogan Page [ ]

IMPROVING EMPLOYEE PERFORMANCE, (CBT), Interactive Learning Systems [ ]

MANAGING PERFORMANCE FOR QUALITY, (Video), Longman Training [ ]

MANAGING PERFORMANCE, (Videos), BBC Training Videos [ ]

MANAGING CREATIVITY, (Video), BBC for Business [ ]

MANAGING AT THE SPEED OF CHANGE, (Video), Melrose [ ]

MANAGING THE POOR PERFORMER, (Book), Valerie and Andrew Stewart, Gower [ ]

PERFORMANCE REVIEW, (Interactive Video), Longman Training [ ]

PLANNING AND MANAGING CHANGE, (Book), Kogan Page with Manchester Open Learning [ ]

PRACTICAL PERFORMANCE APPRAISAL, (Book), Valerie and Andrew Stewart, Gower [ ]

TEACHING THE ELEPHANT TO DANCE, (Book), James A Belasco, Business Books [ ]

THE CREATIVE MANAGER'S POCKETBOOK, (Book), Townsend and Favier, Management Pocketbooks [ ]

THE JOURNEY TO EXCELLENCE, (Video), BBC Training Videos [ ]

MANAGING PERFORMANCE, (Video), Gower [ ]

MANAGING FOR HIGH PERFORMANCE, (Book), Roger Moores, The Industrial Society [ ]

MANAGING FOR PERFORMANCE, (Book), Alasdair White, Piatkus [ ]

PERFORMANCE MANAGEMENT: MANAGING BEST PRACTICE, (Book), The Industrial Society [ ]

CHANGE MANAGEMENT, (Book), The Industrial Society [ ]

Effective Customer Service

A PASSION FOR CUSTOMERS, (Video), Melrose [ ]

COLLEAGUES AS CUSTOMERS, (Video), Fenman Training [ ]

CREATING CUSTOMER LOYALTY, (Book), Kogan Page with Manchester Open Learning [ ]

CUSTOMER SERVICE, (Audiotape), Motivation Cassettes [ ]

CUSTOMER CARE, (Book), Francis Sacker, The Industrial Society [ ]

CUSTOMER CARE, (Book), Sarah Cook, Kogan Page [ ]

HOW TO WIN CUSTOMERS AND KEEP THEM FOR LIFE, (Audiotape), Nightingale-Conant [ ]

KEEPING CUSTOMERS COOL, (Video), Melrose [ ]

LISTENING LEADERS - THE CUSTOMER RESPONSE LOOP, (Video), Video Arts [ ]

MANAGING FOR CUSTOMER CARE, (Video), Fenman Training [ ]

MANAGING QUALITY CUSTOMER SERVICE, (Book), William B Martin, Kogan Page [ ]

MANAGING CUSTOMER SERVICE, (Video),
BBC Training Video [ ]

SECRET SERVICE, (Video), BBC Training Videos [ ]

THE CUSTOMER SERVICE POCKETBOOK, (Book),
Tony Newby, Management Pocketbooks [ ]

THE CUSTOMER-DRIVEN COMPANY, (Book),
Richard C Whiteley, Business Books [ ]

WORKING FOR CUSTOMERS, (Book),
David Bernstein, CBI [ ]

CUSTOMER LOYALTY AND SUCCESS, (Book),
James J Lynch, Macmillan [ ]

BUT I DON'T HAVE CUSTOMERS, (Video), Melrose [ ]

INTERNAL CUSTOMER SERVICE, (Video), Melrose [ ]

CUSTOMER CARE MANAGING BEST PRACTICE,
(Book), The Industrial Society [ ]

DELIGHTING CUSTOMERS, (Book),
Peter Donovan and Timothy Samler,
Chapman and Hall [ ]

SUCCESSFUL CUSTOMER CARE IN A WEEK,
(Book), John H Wellemin, Headway [ ]